Out of the IDE

Out of the IDE: Because the Next Line of Code Won't Be Yours

Published by Root Authority Press

www.rootauthoritypress.com

First edition, 2026

ISBN: 979-8-9955274-0-4

Cover design by the author

Printed in the United States of America

OUT OF THE IDE

Because the Next Line of Code Won't Be Yours

Enrique Somoza, D.Sc.

ROOT AUTHORITY

PRESS

www.rootauthoritypress.com

For every developer who looked up from the screen and wondered what comes next.

FOREWORD

Foreword

I have worked with a lot of engineers over the years. The brilliant ones are easy to spot. They solve problems faster than anyone in the room, write code that makes you rethink what clean architecture actually means, and carry opinions about systems design that are almost always right.

But here is something I have noticed again and again. The most brilliant engineers are not always the most effective ones.

Effectiveness at the senior level requires something that no programming language teaches. It requires the ability to translate what you know into outcomes that other people can see, measure, and act on. It requires the discipline to stop solving every problem yourself and start building environments where problems get solved without you. It requires understanding that your job is no longer to be the smartest person in the room. Your job is to make the room smarter.

Most engineers discover this the hard way. They get promoted into a role where the rules are different, and nobody hands them the new rulebook. They sit in meetings where the best technical argument loses to the best-framed argument. They watch less experienced people gain more influence, and they cannot figure out why. They start to wonder whether leadership is just politics dressed up in a nicer word.

It is not. But it is a skill. And like any skill, it can be learned deliberately or painfully. This book exists so you can choose deliberately.

What Enrique has done here is something I have rarely seen in technical leadership books. He has written from inside the experience, not above it.

The frameworks in these pages are not borrowed from management theory textbooks. They are built from the specific, sometimes uncomfortable reality of being an engineer who realizes that the next problem worth solving is not in the codebase.

Every chapter grounds its ideas in scenarios that will feel familiar. The engineer who had the right solution and watched it get ignored. The team that built the wrong feature because nobody mapped the dependencies. The tech lead who confused being busy with being effective. These are not hypothetical examples. They are Tuesday.

If you are a senior developer, a staff engineer, or a tech lead who has started to sense that something in your career needs to shift, pay attention to this book. Not because it will tell you to stop being technical. Because it will show you how to make your technical depth count in ways you have not tried yet.

The developers who figure this out become the ones who shape products, teams, and companies. The ones who do not keep wondering why nobody listens to them.

Read this book. Do the exercises. Try the Monday morning actions. Give it ninety days. You will not recognize how you operate in meetings, in planning sessions, or in the moments where decisions actually get made.

And you will still be an engineer. Just one who finally learned how to lead.

Contents

Foreword v
Contents vii
When Code Started Writing Itself 1
The Real Shift Is Not About AI 2
The Hidden Gap in Most Developers' Careers 3
My Own Transition 4
The Future Belongs to Meta-Developers 4
What This Book Will Help You Do 5
A Final Thought Before We Begin 6
What Nobody Told You About the Next Five Years 7
The Uncomfortable Math 7
The Productivity Paradox 7
The Junior Squeeze 8
Three Career Trajectories 9
What the Job Postings Are Already Telling You 10
The Middle Tier Compression 11
The Timeline Is Not What You Think 12
What This Book Will Give You 12
Where You Stand Right Now 14
Why This Assessment Matters 14
A Note on Honesty 15
Dimension One: Strategic Thinking 15
Dimension Two: Communication 16
Dimension Three: People Leadership 17
Dimension Four: Systems and Decision-Making 18
Dimension Five: Influence and Organizational Effectiveness 18
Reading Your Results 19
One More Thing 20
Chapter 1: The Changing Landscape 21
The Era of Invisible Code 21
Why Coding Is No Longer the Bottleneck 22
The Value Shift Curve 23

The Myth of the 10x Developer 24
What Most Developers Underestimate About AI 25
Two Developers, Two Outcomes 26
What Most Developers Get Wrong 27
Three Paths Developers Will Take 28
The Opportunity Hidden in the Shift 29
What to Do Monday Morning 30
Checklist: Are You Still Competing on Code? 31
Chapter 2: From Executor to Strategist 32
The Execution Trap 32
Why Execution Alone Stops Working 33
The 4-Level Impact Model 34
Two Engineers, One Feature, Opposite Outcomes 35
What Most Developers Get Wrong About Strategy 36
The Shift from Execution to Strategy 38
Where Careers Slow Down 39
Thinking in Outcomes Instead of Tasks 40
Expanding Influence 41
The Strategic Developer Framework 42
What to Do Monday Morning 43
Checklist: Are You Operating as an Executor or a Strategist? 44
Chapter 3: Communication That Moves Code Without Writing It 46
Trained to Talk to Machines 46
The Translation Layer 47
Right Solution, Wrong Room 49
Same Problem, Different Engineer 50
Why Engineers Struggle in Meetings 51
What Most Developers Get Wrong About Communication 52
The Force Multiplier 53
Meetings as Decision Engines 54
Writing That Creates Alignment 56
What to Do Monday Morning 56
The Cost of Not Communicating 57
Checklist: Are You Communicating for Engineers or for Decisions? 58
Chapter 4: Managing Humans 60
The Shift from Systems to People 60

Why Great Engineers Struggle with People 61
The Human Debugging Model 62
A High Performer Comes Apart 64
A Conflict Becomes a Catalyst 65
What Most Developers Get Wrong About Management 67
Psychological Safety Is Not a Buzzword 68
Giving Feedback That Actually Changes Behavior 69
Running One-on-Ones That Matter 70
What to Do Monday Morning 71
Motivating Different Types of Engineers 72
Checklist: Are You Managing Tasks or People? 73
Chapter 5: Thinking in Systems 75
The Feature Factory 75
Why Feature Thinking Breaks at Scale 76
The System Lens 77
The Feature That Broke the System 78
What Most Developers Miss About Systems 80
Second-Order Effects 81
Trade-offs at Scale 82
Avoiding Local Optimization 83
What to Do Monday Morning 84
Checklist: Are You Solving Locally or System-Wide? 85
Chapter 6: Decision Making Under Uncertainty 87
The Comfortable Illusion of Complete Information 87
Why Engineers Struggle with Ambiguity 88
The 70% Decision Rule 89
Reversible vs Irreversible Decisions 91
When Analysis Becomes Avoidance 92
What Most Developers Get Wrong About Decisions 94
The Courage to Decide and Be Wrong 95
What to Do Monday Morning 95
Checklist: Are You Waiting for Certainty? 96
Chapter 7: Building Influence Without Authority 99
The Person Nobody Invited 99
Influence vs Authority 99
The Influence Triangle 100

The Engineer Nobody Heard ... 102
How Decisions Actually Get Made ... 104
What Most Developers Misunderstand About Influence ... 105
Stakeholder Management as Influence Architecture ... 106
Aligning Engineering, Product, and Leadership ... 108
What to Do Monday Morning ... 109
Checklist: Do People Act on What You Say? ... 110
Chapter 8: The Leadership Toolkit ... 112
From Principles to Practice ... 112
What Most Developers Lack When They Step into Leadership ... 112
Tool One: The Decision Log ... 113
Tool Two: The Stakeholder Map ... 115
Tool Three: Delegation Levels ... 116
Communication Templates ... 118
Creating Visibility Without Self-Promotion ... 119
What to Do Monday Morning ... 120
Checklist: Do You Have a Repeatable System? ... 121
Chapter 9: The Future of Technical Leadership ... 123
The Job That Does Not Exist Yet ... 123
What Changes vs What Does Not ... 124
What Most People Get Wrong About AI ... 125
The Meta-Developer Model ... 126
The Evolving Shape of Engineering Organizations ... 127
Skills That Compound vs Skills That Expire ... 128
What to Do Monday Morning ... 129
Checklist: Are You Adapting or Reacting? ... 130
Chapter 10: The Developer Manifesto ... 132
What This Book Was Really About ... 132
Stop Optimizing for Code. Start Optimizing for Outcomes. ... 132
Clarity Creates Influence. ... 133
The Best Decision Available Now Beats the Perfect Decision Eventually. ... 133
Translate, Do Not Explain. ... 134
Systems Are Bigger Than Software ... 134
People Are Not Bugs to Fix. ... 135
Influence Is Earned in Inches. ... 135
Your Reputation Is Your Résumé. ... 136

Own More Than You Were Assigned......136
Build for the Long Term......136
The Next Line of Code......137
A Note to the Developer Reading This at 2 AM......139
A Note to the Developer Reading This at 2 AM......139
Acknowledgments......142
Chapter Exercises......143
How to Use These Exercises......143
Chapter 1: The Changing Landscape......143
Chapter 2: From Executor to Strategist......144
Chapter 3: Communication as a Force Multiplier......145
Chapter 4: Managing Humans......146
Chapter 5: Thinking in Systems......147
Chapter 6: Decision-Making Under Uncertainty......148
Chapter 7: Building Influence Without Authority......149
Chapter 8: The Leadership Toolkit......149
Chapter 9: The Future of Technical Leadership......150
Chapter 10: The Developer Leadership Manifesto......151
Your First 90 Days......153
Why Ninety Days......153
Month One: Observe and Map......153
The Observation Trap......155
Month Two: Experiment and Practice......155
What If the Experiments Fail?......156
Month Three: Build Systems and Habits......156
After the Ninety Days......157
Frameworks Quick Reference......159
How to Use This Reference......159
The Four-Question Strategic Filter (Chapter 2)......159
The Three Levels of Communication (Chapter 3)......160
The Feedback Framework (Chapter 4)......160
The One-on-One Template (Chapter 4)......161
The Second-Order Effects Map (Chapter 5)......161
The Decision Classification Matrix (Chapter 6)......162
The Stakeholder Map (Chapter 7)......162
The Three Delegation Buckets (Chapter 8)......163

The Four Communication Templates (Chapter 8)....163
The Visibility Framework (Chapter 8)....164
Annotated Reading List 165
About This List....165
Strategic Thinking (Chapters 1 and 2)....165
Communication (Chapter 3)....166
People Leadership (Chapter 4)....166
Systems Thinking and Decision-Making (Chapters 5 and 6)....167
Influence and Organizational Dynamics (Chapters 7 and 8)....167
The Future of Technical Work (Chapter 9)....168
Where to Start....168
About the Author 169

INTRODUCTION

When Code Started Writing Itself

For most of the past fifty years, being a great developer meant one thing: **you could write better code than the person next to you.**

You knew the language deeper. You understood the framework better. You debugged faster. You shipped cleaner architecture.

The industry rewarded that skill. Promotions, recognition, influence inside organizations. The best engineers became senior engineers, then architects, and eventually technical leaders.

And the entire system worked because one assumption held true:

Writing code was hard.

Then something changed.

Almost overnight, developers around the world started noticing something strange in their editors. A function would appear before they finished typing. An entire API endpoint would materialize from a comment. A complex regex would show up perfectly formatted, written in seconds by a machine that had never attended a stand-up meeting or argued about tabs versus spaces.

At first it felt like magic.

Then it started to feel like a warning.

GitHub Copilot. Large language models. AI agents that could generate entire services, refactor codebases, and explain architecture decisions faster than most humans could read documentation.

The tools kept improving. Every month the suggestions became more accurate, more complete, and more confident.

Developers began asking a question that had never really existed before.

If AI can write the code, what exactly is my job?

For some people, the reaction was excitement. The idea of writing less boilerplate and shipping faster sounded like a dream.

For others, it triggered something closer to quiet anxiety.

Because deep down, many developers had built their professional identity around one core belief:

My value comes from the code I produce.

And suddenly the industry was shifting toward a reality where producing code might become the least valuable part of the job.

This book is not about resisting that shift.

It is about understanding it.

And more importantly, staying relevant inside it.

The Real Shift Is Not About AI

Most discussions about AI and software development focus on the wrong problem.

They debate whether machines will replace developers. They compare benchmarks and model capabilities. They argue about whether code generated by AI is "good enough."

But those conversations miss the deeper change happening underneath the surface.

The real shift is not that machines can write code.

The real shift is that coding itself is becoming a smaller part of creating value in technology.

Think about the work that actually determines whether a product succeeds.

Someone has to define the problem. Someone has to decide which features matter. Someone has to prioritize trade-offs between performance, reliability, and speed. Someone has to align engineers, product managers, executives, designers, and customers around a shared outcome.

None of those problems are solved by writing another function.

They are solved by thinking, communicating, and leading.

For years, many developers avoided those responsibilities because they could still create massive value purely through technical execution.

But as AI accelerates the execution layer of software development, the center of gravity in our profession is shifting upward.

The developers who thrive in the next decade will not simply be the ones who code faster. They will be the ones who can connect technology to outcomes. They will understand systems, organizations, incentives, and trade-offs.

In other words, they will think more like leaders.

The Hidden Gap in Most Developers' Careers

Here is the uncomfortable truth most engineers discover late in their careers.

Software engineering teaches you how to build systems. It does not teach you how to lead people.

Developers spend years mastering algorithms, frameworks, architecture patterns, debugging techniques, and performance optimization. But very few are trained in influencing decisions, communicating with executives, navigating organizational dynamics, aligning teams around strategy, or turning ambiguity into clear direction.

So when engineers move into senior roles, staff roles, or management positions, many feel like they have been dropped into an entirely different profession.

Because in many ways, they have.

The job stops being about writing code yourself and becomes about creating the conditions where great code gets written.

That requires a completely different skill set.

And unfortunately, most developers are forced to figure those skills out the hard way. Through mistakes. Through awkward meetings. Through projects that fail not because the code was wrong, but because the communication was.

My Own Transition

Early in my career, I believed the same thing many developers believe.

If I could just become technically strong enough, everything else would take care of itself.

And for a while, that approach worked.

But eventually I started noticing something strange. The engineers who had the biggest impact inside organizations were not always the ones writing the most sophisticated code.

They were the ones asking the right questions.

They were the ones clarifying ambiguous problems. They were the ones translating complex technical ideas into decisions that executives could understand. They influenced roadmaps. They shaped strategy. They aligned teams.

In many cases, they wrote less code than everyone else.

But their impact was far greater.

It took me years to realize why. They had learned a skill that most developers never consciously practice:

They knew how to turn technical knowledge into influence.

That realization changed how I approached my career. Instead of focusing exclusively on becoming a better engineer, I started focusing on becoming a better communicator, decision-maker, and leader.

Ironically, those skills ended up amplifying my technical background rather than replacing it. Because once you understand both the technical layer and the human layer of building systems, you can operate at a completely different level.

The Future Belongs to Meta-Developers

In the coming years, the most valuable people in software will not simply be developers.

They will be what I like to call meta-developers.

People who understand code deeply, but whose primary value comes from orchestrating systems, teams, and outcomes. They will use AI tools instead of competing with them. They will focus less on writing individual functions and more on designing environments where great solutions emerge. They will guide decisions, shape architecture, and align organizations around meaningful goals.

In other words, they will move out of the IDE and into the larger system that surrounds it.

That transition can feel uncomfortable at first. Developers often worry that moving toward leadership means abandoning the craft they love.

But the reality is the opposite.

The best technical leaders never stop thinking like engineers. They simply expand the scope of the problems they solve. Instead of debugging code, they debug organizations. Instead of designing classes and services, they design systems of collaboration. Instead of optimizing algorithms, they optimize decision-making.

What This Book Will Help You Do

This book is designed to help developers make that transition deliberately instead of accidentally.

Inside these chapters, we will explore how the role of developers is evolving in the age of AI, why communication is becoming the most valuable technical skill, how to think like a strategist instead of an executor, how to manage people not just repositories, how to build influence inside organizations, and how to make decisions when the answers are unclear.

None of this requires you to stop being technical.

In fact, your technical background is your biggest advantage.

The goal is not to replace your engineering mindset. The goal is to expand it.

A Final Thought Before We Begin

Software development has always been about solving problems.

For decades, those problems mostly lived inside code. But the problems that define the future of technology are much larger. They involve people. Organizations. Markets. Ethics. Strategy.

The developers who learn to navigate those systems will shape the next era of the industry. The ones who remain focused only on the syntax layer will eventually find themselves competing with tools that can generate that syntax faster than they can type.

This book is not a eulogy for developers.

It is a guide for evolution.

Because the next line of code might not be written by you. But the next important decision still will be.

BEFORE WE BEGIN

What Nobody Told You About the Next Five Years

The Uncomfortable Math

Before we go any further, you deserve the honest version.

Not the LinkedIn version where every disruption is an opportunity and every threat is actually a gift. Not the conference keynote version where someone who has not written production code in a decade tells you to embrace the change. The version built on numbers and patterns that are already visible if you know where to look.

The software industry is about to go through a compression that will reshape careers in ways most developers are not prepared for. Not because AI is going to replace all developers tomorrow. That framing is lazy and inaccurate. But because the economics of software production are shifting fast enough that the roles, expectations, and career paths you have built your plans around will look fundamentally different within five years.

Here is what the data is already telling us.

The Productivity Paradox

In 2023, McKinsey published research showing that AI coding assistants could increase developer productivity by 25 to 50 percent on common tasks. GitHub's own data suggested that Copilot users completed tasks 55 percent faster than those without it. By 2025, those numbers had improved again.

At first glance, this looks like good news. You get more done in less time. You ship faster. You spend less time on boilerplate.

But here is the part that most productivity narratives leave out.

When individual productivity rises dramatically, organizations do not simply celebrate and keep headcount the same. They recalculate. If one developer with AI assistance can do what two developers did before, the math gets uncomfortable quickly.

This does not mean mass layoffs are inevitable. But it does mean that the bar for what justifies a senior developer salary is moving. The question is no longer whether you can write good code. The question is whether you can do things that AI-assisted junior developers cannot.

And right now, a lot of experienced developers cannot clearly articulate what those things are.

This is not a hypothetical concern. It is an active conversation happening in boardrooms and budget meetings at companies of every size. Engineering leaders are looking at their headcount, looking at their AI tool adoption metrics, and asking a question that would have been unthinkable three years ago: do we need this many developers to ship what we need to ship?

The honest answer, increasingly, is no. Not because the developers are not talented. But because the definition of what requires human talent is getting narrower.

The Junior Squeeze

The first wave of impact is already hitting entry-level roles. Companies that used to hire ten junior developers to handle implementation work are discovering that three mid-level developers with AI tools can cover the same output. Internship programs are shrinking. Boot camp placement rates are dropping. The traditional entry point into the industry, writing code under supervision, is getting narrower every year.

This matters for senior developers too, even if it does not feel like it yet. The pipeline that feeds your team is thinning. The mentorship models you grew up with are changing. And the skills that once separated a junior from a senior, speed, language fluency, pattern recognition in code, are exactly the skills where AI is closing the gap fastest.

The gap that AI cannot close is judgment. Knowing what to build, who to talk to, how to prioritize competing demands, when to push back on a requirement, how to align a team around an outcome. These are the skills that become more valuable as code production gets cheaper. But they are also the skills that most technical career paths never explicitly develop.

Think about your own career for a moment. How many hours have you invested in learning new languages, frameworks, and tools? Now compare that to how many hours you have invested in learning to communicate a technical trade-off to a non-technical stakeholder. Or how to run a meeting that actually produces a decision. Or how to build alignment across teams that have competing priorities.

If the ratio is heavily skewed toward the technical side, you are not unusual. You are normal. The industry trained you this way. But normal is exactly the problem when the ground is shifting.

Three Career Trajectories

When you look at how the industry is reorganizing, three distinct paths are emerging for experienced developers. Not everyone will choose consciously. Many will drift into one of these paths without realizing it.

The first path is the specialist. These are developers who go deep into areas where AI assistance is still limited. Security, performance engineering, distributed systems architecture, machine learning infrastructure. Domains where the problems are genuinely hard and the cost of getting it wrong is high enough that organizations will pay a premium for human expertise. This path is viable but narrow. It requires continuous investment in increasingly specialized knowledge, and the window of AI limitation in any given domain tends to shrink over time.

The second path is the integrator. These developers become the bridge between AI capabilities and organizational needs. They understand the tools well enough to orchestrate them, evaluate their output, and design systems that combine human and machine contributions effectively. Think of it as being the person who directs the AI rather than competes with it. This is a growing path, but it carries its own risk. If your value is primarily in using AI tools effectively, you are one product update away from having that value automated.

The third path is the leader. Not in the sense of having a management title, though that is one version of it. In the sense of being the person who defines what gets built, why it matters, how teams should be organized to build it, and what success looks like when it ships. This is the path with the most durable value because it requires the skills that are hardest to automate: communication, judgment, influence, and the ability to navigate organizational complexity.

This book is about the third path.

Not because the other two are invalid. They are legitimate choices for the right people at the right time. But the third path is the one with the widest margin of safety and the longest career runway. It is also the one that the fewest developers are preparing for.

What the Job Postings Are Already Telling You

If you want to see the future, read job descriptions. Not for what they say explicitly, but for how the requirements have shifted.

Five years ago, a senior developer job posting was 80 percent technical requirements. Specific languages, frameworks, years of experience with particular tools. The remaining 20 percent was generic soft skills language that nobody took seriously.

Today, the ratio is changing. Senior and staff engineer postings increasingly list requirements like: ability to influence technical direction across teams, experience driving alignment between engineering and product, track record of mentoring and developing other engineers, ability to communicate technical trade-offs to non-technical stakeholders.

These are not soft skills in the traditional sense. They are leadership skills. And the market is pricing them in because organizations have learned, sometimes painfully, that technical excellence without organizational effectiveness produces teams that build impressive things nobody asked for.

The developers who read this shift correctly and invest in these capabilities now will have a significant advantage. The developers who assume their technical depth alone will carry them forward are making a bet that gets riskier every year.

This is not about abandoning technical excellence. It is about recognizing that technical excellence is necessary but no longer sufficient. The bar has moved. And the job market is the most honest signal available about where it has moved to.

The Middle Tier Compression

There is a specific career stage where the risk is highest, and most people in it do not see it yet.

If you are a mid-to-senior developer whose primary value proposition is reliable implementation of well-defined features, you are in the compression zone. Not because you are bad at your job. You might be excellent at it. But because well-defined implementation is exactly the category where AI assistance is most effective.

The compression works like this. Junior developers with AI tools start handling tasks that used to require mid-level experience. Senior developers with AI tools start handling tasks that used to require a team. The middle tier, the reliable implementers, face pressure from both directions simultaneously.

This is not speculation. It is the pattern that has already played out in other industries when automation hit the middle of the skill curve. Data entry, basic accounting, routine legal research. The entry-level roles got eliminated or transformed. The expert roles became more valuable. And the middle tier, the people who were good but not exceptional, faced the hardest transition.

In software, the compression is happening faster because the tools are improving faster than anyone expected. And the developers who will navigate it successfully are the ones who move up the value chain before the compression forces them to.

Moving up the value chain does not mean moving away from technology. It means moving toward the decisions that determine how technology gets used. It means becoming the person who shapes what gets built, not just the person who builds what someone else shaped. It means trading the comfort of clear technical problems for the discomfort of ambiguous organizational ones.

That trade is not easy. But it is the trade that creates career resilience in a market where pure implementation skill is becoming a commodity.

The Timeline Is Not What You Think

Most developers assume they have years to figure this out. The technology is not that good yet, they reason. My company is slow to adopt new tools. The really hard problems still need humans.

All three of those statements are true today. None of them will be true in the same way in 2028 or 2029.

The adoption curve for AI coding tools is steeper than any previous developer tool category. It took years for version control, containerization, and cloud infrastructure to reach mainstream adoption. AI coding assistants went from novelty to standard practice in under two years. The next wave, AI agents that can handle multi-step engineering tasks, is already in production at major companies.

This does not mean you need to panic. Panic is the least useful response to structural change. But it does mean that the window for proactive career investment is shorter than it feels. The best time to develop leadership capabilities was two years ago. The second-best time is right now.

Because the developers who wait until the compression reaches their role will be developing these skills from a position of weakness. They will be competing for leadership opportunities with people who started preparing earlier. They will be learning to communicate, influence, and think strategically while also dealing with the stress of career uncertainty.

The developers who start now will be developing these skills from a position of strength. They still have credibility, time, and the luxury of learning through practice rather than desperation.

That difference, between learning from strength and learning from desperation, is the difference between career growth and career survival. Both are possible. But only one of them feels like a choice you made rather than a situation that was forced on you.

What This Book Will Give You

The next ten chapters are not theoretical. They are built around the specific capabilities that separate developers who thrive through industry transitions from developers who get caught in them.

You will learn to think strategically instead of just tactically. To communicate in ways that create alignment and influence decisions. To manage people and navigate the organizational dynamics that determine which technical work actually gets funded and supported. To make decisions under uncertainty. To build influence without authority. To use practical tools and frameworks that translate these concepts into daily action.

None of this requires you to stop being technical. The developers who lead most effectively are deeply technical. Their credibility comes from understanding the systems they are helping to direct. The goal is not to abandon your technical identity. It is to expand it.

The best technical leaders are not former developers who forgot how to code. They are active developers who learned how to do everything else. They can review a pull request in the morning, realign a product roadmap before lunch, and resolve a cross-team dependency conflict in the afternoon. They do this not because they are superhuman but because they understand that technical skill and organizational skill are not separate tracks. They are layers of the same job.

If that sounds like a lot, it is. Leadership is harder than coding. Anyone who tells you otherwise is selling something or has never done both. But it is also more durable, more impactful, and, once you develop the skills, more rewarding than optimizing a function that an AI will rewrite next quarter anyway.

But first, you need to know where you stand. The next section will help you assess where your current capabilities are strong and where the gaps are that this book can help you close. Be honest with yourself. The assessment is only useful if you are.

The market does not care about your intentions. It cares about your capabilities. And the capabilities that matter are changing faster than most people want to admit.

SELF-ASSESSMENT

Where You Stand Right Now

Why This Assessment Matters

Most developers have a reasonably accurate picture of their technical capabilities. You know which languages you are strong in. You know whether your system design skills are solid or shaky. You probably have a decent sense of where you rank among the engineers you have worked with.

But when it comes to the capabilities this book addresses, most developers are operating blind. Not because the skills are invisible. Because nobody ever asked you to evaluate them.

Nobody sat you down during a performance review and said, "Let us talk about how effectively you translate technical complexity for non-technical stakeholders." Nobody measured your ability to run a meeting that produces a decision instead of a discussion. Nobody tracked whether your influence on cross-team decisions increased or decreased over the past year.

So you do not have a baseline. And without a baseline, growth is just guessing.

This assessment gives you that baseline. It covers five dimensions that correspond to the core sections of this book. For each dimension, you will rate yourself honestly and identify specific gaps. The goal is not to produce a score. Scores are satisfying but useless. The goal is to produce clarity about where to focus your energy as you read the chapters ahead.

Be honest. Nobody is grading this. The only person who loses when you inflate your self-assessment is you.

A Note on Honesty

Self-assessment is hard for developers. We are trained to evaluate objectively. We can tell you whether a function is O(n) or O(n log n). We can benchmark a system and report the results without bias.

But when the system being evaluated is ourselves, objectivity disappears. We anchor on our best moments instead of our typical behavior. We rate ourselves based on what we know we should do rather than what we actually do. We assume that understanding a concept is the same as practicing it.

It is not.

For each statement in the dimensions below, answer based on your behavior in the last three months. Not what you believe you could do. Not what you plan to do. What you have actually done. The distinction matters. A lot of developers know they should communicate more clearly with stakeholders. Far fewer have actually changed how they communicate in the last quarter.

Answer honestly. The self-assessment is only as useful as the truth you put into it.

Dimension One: Strategic Thinking

This dimension measures whether you think in outcomes or tasks. Whether you understand why something is being built, not just what is being built. Whether you can connect daily work to broader organizational goals.

Rate yourself on each statement. Use a simple scale: rarely, sometimes, or consistently.

Before starting a new project or feature, I can clearly articulate what business outcome it is meant to produce.

When I receive a requirement I disagree with, I push back with an alternative that addresses the same underlying goal rather than just objecting.

I can explain to a non-technical person why a particular technical decision matters for the product or the business.

When prioritizing my work, I consider impact on organizational goals rather than just technical urgency or ticket order.

I regularly think about what should not be built, not just what should be.

If you answered "rarely" or "sometimes" to three or more of these, Chapter 2 should be a priority. The shift from executor to strategist is the foundation that everything else builds on. Without it, the other skills operate at reduced effectiveness because you are applying them to the wrong problems.

If you answered "consistently" to most of these, pay attention to the nuances in Chapter 2 anyway. There is a significant difference between understanding strategic thinking conceptually and practicing it under pressure when deadlines are tight and stakeholders are impatient.

Dimension Two: Communication

This dimension measures your ability to translate, align, and influence through how you share information. Not your personality or charisma. Your effectiveness at getting the right information to the right people in the right form.

Rate yourself on each statement.

When I write a technical document or proposal, the reader can act on it without asking me follow-up questions.

I adjust my communication style based on the audience. I explain things differently to engineers, product managers, and executives.

In meetings, I speak up when I have relevant input rather than waiting to be asked or staying silent.

When I disagree with a decision, I express my disagreement clearly and constructively rather than going along passively or complaining afterward.

I can summarize a complex technical situation in three sentences or fewer without losing the essential information.

If this dimension is weak, Chapter 3 is where you should slow down and practice the exercises. Communication is the force multiplier. Every other leadership skill is bottlenecked by your ability to express it clearly. A brilliant strategic insight that you cannot communicate is indistinguishable from not having the insight at all.

Pay particular attention to the gap between what you think you communicate and what other people actually hear. Most developers overestimate their communication effectiveness because they are evaluating clarity from their own perspective rather than the receiver's.

Dimension Three: People Leadership

This dimension measures your ability to work through people rather than around them. To create conditions where others do their best work. To handle the messy, ambiguous, emotionally complex reality of managing human beings.

Rate yourself on each statement.

I can give direct, specific feedback to a colleague about their work without the conversation becoming defensive or uncomfortable.

When someone on my team is underperforming, I address it directly rather than working around them or hoping it resolves itself.

I understand what motivates the individuals I work with and I adjust my approach accordingly rather than treating everyone the same way.

I can facilitate a productive one-on-one conversation that surfaces real concerns rather than surface-level status updates.

When team dynamics are off, I notice the signs and take action rather than assuming it will sort itself out.

This is typically the weakest dimension for developers making the leadership transition. Not because developers are bad with people. Because the industry has never required them to be good with people in a structured, intentional way. Writing code is a solitary skill. Leading people is a relational one. The mental models are completely different.

If this dimension is weak, Chapters 4 and 7 are your highest-leverage reading. But also recognize that people skills develop through practice, not through reading. You will need to put yourself in situations that feel uncomfortable. The first awkward feedback conversation is the price of admission.

Dimension Four: Systems and Decision-Making

This dimension combines two related capabilities: thinking in systems (understanding second-order effects, dependencies, and trade-offs at scale) and making decisions under uncertainty (moving forward with imperfect information and accepting the consequences).

Rate yourself on each statement.

When evaluating a technical decision, I consider its impact on adjacent teams and systems, not just my immediate scope.

I can identify when a short-term solution will create long-term problems and I raise that concern even when the team wants to move fast.

When I do not have complete information, I can still make a decision and commit to it rather than delaying until certainty is available.

I distinguish between reversible and irreversible decisions and I allocate my analysis time accordingly.

When a decision I made turns out to be wrong, I acknowledge it quickly and change course rather than defending the original choice.

I can explain the trade-offs of a technical approach in terms that non-engineers understand and care about.

If this dimension is weak, Chapters 5 and 6 are essential. Systems thinking and decision-making are the capabilities that separate senior developers from actual leaders. A senior developer can build a good system. A leader can evaluate whether that system should exist at all and make that call when the evidence is ambiguous.

Most developers are more comfortable with systems thinking than with decision-making under uncertainty. The systems part is an extension of engineering thinking. The decision part requires a fundamentally different relationship with risk and imperfection.

Dimension Five: Influence and Organizational Effectiveness

This dimension measures your ability to operate within an organization as a political and social system. Not politics in the cynical sense. Politics in the sense of understanding how decisions actually get made, who has power, how to navigate competing interests, and how to ensure that good technical work gets supported and funded.

Rate yourself on each statement.

I know who the key decision-makers are for the projects that affect my work, and I have relationships with them.

When I want to change how something is done, I build support before proposing the change rather than presenting it cold and hoping the argument is strong enough.

I can navigate disagreements between engineering and product or engineering and leadership without creating adversarial dynamics.

My work is visible to people outside my immediate team. Stakeholders and leaders know what I contribute.

I have been able to influence a significant decision even when I did not have formal authority over it.

If this dimension is weak, Chapters 7 and 8 are where you should invest the most attention. Influence is the skill that converts all the other skills into career results. You can think strategically, communicate clearly, lead people well, and make good decisions, but if nobody with power knows about it, the career impact is minimal.

This is the dimension that makes many engineers uncomfortable. It feels like self-promotion or manipulation. It is neither. It is the practical reality of how organizations work. Ideas do not win on merit alone. They win when the right people understand them and trust the person presenting them.

Reading Your Results

Look at the pattern across all five dimensions. Most people will find one or two dimensions that are clearly weaker than the others. Those are your priority chapters.

But also pay attention to the dimension you rated highest. Overconfidence in your strongest area is one of the most common blind spots. The developer who thinks they communicate well often has never received honest feedback about how their communication lands. The developer who thinks they are a strong systems thinker might be confusing technical architecture with organizational systems thinking.

A useful exercise: after completing this self-assessment, share it with someone you trust. A manager, a peer you respect, a mentor. Ask them to rate you on the same statements. The gap between your self-assessment and their assessment is the most valuable data you will collect from this exercise.

That gap is where the real growth opportunity lives. Not in the dimensions you already know are weak. In the dimensions where you think you are strong but the people around you see it differently.

Keep your results somewhere accessible. After finishing the book and working through the exercises, come back to this assessment. The comparison between your answers now and your answers then will tell you more about your growth than any external metric could.

One More Thing

It is tempting to read through this assessment quickly, give yourself generous ratings, and move on to the chapters. Resist that temptation.

The developers who get the most out of this book are the ones who start with an honest accounting of where they are. Not where they wish they were. Not where they think they should be at their career stage. Where they actually are today, based on evidence and behavior rather than intention and self-image.

The chapters ahead will give you specific, practical tools for closing the gaps you just identified. But the tools only work if you know which gaps to apply them to.

Start there. The rest will follow.

CHAPTER 1

The Changing Landscape

The Era of Invisible Code

The moment it hit was a Tuesday afternoon, during a code review.

A developer with eighteen months of experience had submitted a pull request for a feature you estimated would take three days. She had done it in four hours. You opened the diff expecting to find shortcuts, missed edge cases, the usual marks of inexperience. Instead the code was clean. The architecture was sound. The tests covered the important paths. It was not just acceptable. It was good.

You approved it and closed the tab. Then you sat there for a minute, staring at nothing, doing the math in your head. Four hours. She had used an AI coding assistant for most of it. The tool handled the scaffolding, the boilerplate, the test structure. She handled the decisions about what to build and how to organize it. And the result was indistinguishable from what you would have produced yourself, given three days.

That was the moment the ground shifted. Not when you read the headline about AI replacing developers. Not when your company announced its AI strategy. When a junior developer on your own team shipped work that matched your output, at a fraction of the time, because a tool closed the gap that years of experience used to fill.

You are not alone in that moment. It is happening in engineering teams everywhere. And the developers who are honest with themselves know exactly what it means.

This is not a hypothetical. In March 2024, Cognition Labs demonstrated Devin, an AI software engineer that could take a GitHub issue, plan an implementation, write the code, debug failures, and submit a working pull request. Not a toy demo. Production-level work across real repositories. A team at a mid-stage fintech company reported that their AI-assisted pipeline handled 40 percent of their routine backend tickets end to end, from issue to merged PR, with a senior engineer reviewing the output instead of writing it. The engineer's role did not disappear. It transformed. She went from writing code eight hours a day to reviewing, directing, and deciding for six hours and writing code for two.

That ratio is going to keep shifting. And it changes what it means to be valuable.

Why Coding Is No Longer the Bottleneck

For most of us, writing code was the thing. It was the craft we spent years sharpening. We learned languages the way musicians learn instruments. Not just the syntax but the idioms, the patterns, the elegant solutions that separated experienced developers from beginners. That knowledge mattered. It was the foundation of our identity and our market value.

Now the floor is moving.

AI-assisted development tools are not replacing developers. That framing misses the point entirely. What they are doing is compressing the distance between intent and implementation. The gap between "I know what I want to build" and "here is working code that does it" is shrinking fast. When that gap shrinks, the value of being the person who bridges it shrinks too.

Think about what actually happens when you use an AI coding assistant effectively. You describe a problem. You specify constraints. You evaluate the output, identify what is wrong, and redirect. You make judgment calls about architecture, naming, edge cases, and trade-offs. You decide what to build and why.

The tool handles the typing.

That workflow looks a lot less like programming and a lot more like directing. You are still technical. You still need to understand systems deeply. But the nature of your contribution is shifting from production to judgment.

Ask any experienced developer what kills projects. You will hear the same answers over and over. Unclear requirements. Shifting priorities. Teams building the wrong thing. Poor communication between engineering and product. Technical debt that nobody wants to own. Decisions made by people who do not understand the constraints. Leaders who optimize for speed over sustainability.

Notice what is missing from that list. Nobody says, "We failed because we could not write the code."

The ability to produce working software has almost never been the binding constraint on a team's success. The constraint has always been upstream. Understanding the problem correctly. Making good decisions about what to build. Communicating effectively across disciplines. Aligning people around a shared direction.

AI makes this even more stark. As the cost of producing code approaches zero, the relative cost of everything else goes up. Getting requirements right matters more when you can spin up a wrong implementation in hours instead of weeks. Making good architectural decisions matters more when the tool will happily generate a fragile system just as quickly as a resilient one. Communicating clearly with stakeholders matters more when the pace of delivery means misalignment compounds faster.

The bottleneck was never code. It was always judgment, communication, and alignment. AI just made that impossible to ignore.

The Value Shift Curve

There is a simple way to think about where developer value is heading. Call it the Value Shift Curve. It has four stages, each one further from the keyboard and closer to organizational impact.

Stage one is Coding. Writing, debugging, and shipping working software. This is where most developers start and where many stay. It is real, necessary work. But it is the layer AI is compressing fastest. When a tool can scaffold an entire service from a description, the developer whose primary output is code is competing directly with a machine that does not sleep, does not take vacations, and gets better every quarter.

Stage two is Context. Understanding why code exists, not just how it works. This means knowing the business domain, the user problem, the regulatory constraints, the history of decisions that shaped the current system.

Context is what lets you tell the difference between code that is technically correct and code that is actually right. AI can generate solutions. It cannot evaluate whether those solutions fit a situation it does not understand.

Stage three is Decisions. Choosing what to build, what to defer, what to kill. This is where technical knowledge meets strategic thinking. A developer operating at this stage does not just execute. They shape the direction of the product and the team. They weigh trade-offs that involve engineering cost, market timing, organizational capacity, and technical risk simultaneously. This is rare, valuable, and almost impossible to automate.

Stage four is Influence. Aligning people, teams, and organizations around a shared technical direction. Influence means your judgment scales beyond your own hands. You do not have to write the code or even review it. You set the standards, the priorities, and the culture that determine what a team of fifty people builds over the next year. Influence is the least technical stage and the highest leverage one.

Most developers operate between stages one and two. The developers who get promoted fastest operate at stage three. The ones who end up in VP and CTO roles operate at stage four. And here is the uncomfortable part. AI is pushing the floor up. What used to be a comfortable career at stage one is becoming a treadmill. The baseline is rising. If you are not deliberately moving up the curve, the curve is moving under you.

The question is not whether this shift is happening. It is whether you are ahead of it or behind it.

The Myth of the 10x Developer

For decades, the software industry worshipped a particular archetype. The developer who could produce ten times the output of their peers. The 10x developer. The one who could hold an entire system in their head, write code faster than anyone else, and solve problems that stumped the rest of the team.

That archetype was always more complicated than the mythology suggested. The original studies that spawned the idea measured productivity differences across developers but never cleanly defined what "productivity" meant. Lines of code? Features shipped? Problems solved? The metric was always fuzzy. But the legend stuck because it felt true. We all knew someone who seemed to operate on a different level.

Here is what the 10x mythology got wrong. It measured the wrong dimension of value.

Speed of code production was never the primary bottleneck in software development. The developer who could write a sorting algorithm in fifteen minutes instead of an hour was impressive. But the developer who figured out that the team was building the wrong feature entirely was worth more. Even if they typed slowly.

AI makes this distinction impossible to ignore. When a tool can generate boilerplate in seconds, scaffold an entire application from a description, write tests and refactor code on command, raw coding speed stops being a differentiator. The playing field for code production is leveling in a way it never has before.

This does not mean technical depth is irrelevant. Understanding how systems work, why certain architectures fail at scale, where abstractions leak. That knowledge becomes more important when the cost of producing code drops, not less. Anyone can generate code. Knowing whether that code is the right code, whether it will hold up under load, whether it introduces subtle dependencies that will hurt you in six months. That requires experience and judgment that no autocomplete tool provides.

The 10x developer of the next decade will not be ten times faster at writing code. They will be ten times better at knowing what to build, why to build it, and how to get an organization aligned around the right priorities.

That is a fundamentally different skill set. And it is what the Value Shift Curve predicts. The multiplier moves from stage one to stages three and four.

What Most Developers Underestimate About AI

There is a pattern in how developers react to AI coding tools. First, dismissal. “It only generates boilerplate.” Then, cautious adoption. “It is useful for simple things.” Then, a quiet recalibration when they realize the tool is getting better faster than they expected.

Most developers underestimate three things.

The first is the pace of improvement. The gap between what AI could generate in 2022 and what it generates in 2026 is enormous. Models went from producing plausible-looking code that failed at runtime to generating working, tested, deployable features from natural language descriptions. That improvement curve has not flattened. If your mental model of AI capability is based on your last interaction six months ago, your model is already wrong.

The second is the organizational response. When individual productivity rises 40 to 60 percent, companies do not just celebrate and keep headcount the same. They recalculate. Teams that needed eight developers can ship with five. That does not necessarily mean layoffs. It often means fewer new hires, smaller teams taking on bigger scope, and a rising bar for what justifies a senior salary. The math is not about whether AI replaces developers. It is about whether AI changes what a developer is expected to deliver per dollar of compensation.

The third, and most important, is the shift in what gets valued. When code production is cheap, the people who can produce code lose negotiating power. The people who can decide what code should be produced gain it. If your performance reviews are built around pull requests merged, tickets closed, and features shipped, you are being evaluated on a metric that is deflating. The developers who figure out how to demonstrate value in terms of decisions made, risks identified, alignment created, and direction set will end up in very different positions than those who keep optimizing for output volume.

This is not pessimism. It is pattern recognition. And the pattern is clear.

Two Developers, Two Outcomes

Consider two engineers at the same company, same level, same team. Both senior. Both strong technically. Both aware that AI is changing the landscape.

The first, call him Dev A, responds by becoming the best AI operator on the team. He masters his tools. He triples his output. His ticket velocity becomes legendary. Management loves the numbers. He is producing more code than anyone, and it is good code. He becomes the go-to person for fast execution.

The second, call her Dev B, takes a different approach. She starts attending product meetings. Not because she was invited but because she asked. She spends time understanding why features are prioritized the way they are. She starts flagging technical decisions that have business implications the product team has not considered. She rewrites a proposal that was heading toward a six-month build and suggests a phased approach that delivers the core value in six weeks. She uses AI tools too, but mostly to free up time for the work she is doing upstream.

Twelve months later, the company reorganizes. Dev A's team is consolidated. His extraordinary output was real, but the team now needs fewer people to maintain the same throughput because the tools caught up to his workflows. His 3x productivity becomes the new 1x. He is still employed, still respected, but the gap between him and a mid-level engineer with good AI skills has narrowed to the point where his seniority premium is hard to justify.

Dev B gets promoted to Staff Engineer. Not because she wrote more code but because leadership recognized that her judgment saved two product cycles and prevented a costly architectural mistake. Her value was not in what she produced. It was in what she prevented, what she redirected, and what she made possible for others.

Same starting point. Different curve positions. Opposite trajectories.

What Most Developers Get Wrong

The most common mistake developers make in this transition is assuming that "getting better" means going deeper technically. Learning the new framework. Picking up another language. Optimizing their development environment. These are comfortable moves because they feel productive and they fit the identity most developers have built.

But they are horizontal moves at stage one of the Value Shift Curve.

Going deeper at the coding layer when the value floor of that layer is rising is like running faster on a treadmill. You are working harder and staying in the same place relative to the market.

The second mistake is waiting for permission. Developers expect the career ladder, the manager, or the organization to tell them when it is time to shift. That signal is rarely explicit. By the time a company restructures its engineering org or updates its promotion criteria, the developers who moved early are already operating at the next level. The ones who waited are scrambling to catch up.

The third mistake is treating leadership skills as a personality trait rather than a practice. "I am not a people person." "I am an introvert." "I am not political." These are not permanent conditions. They are descriptions of your current comfort zone. Communication, influence, and strategic thinking are skills. They respond to deliberate practice the same way debugging or system design does. The developers who dismiss them as innate qualities they lack are choosing not to compete in the dimension that matters most.

Three Paths Developers Will Take

As AI reshapes what it means to be a developer, the profession is branching into three distinct paths. None of them is wrong. But they lead to very different places. And the choice, whether deliberate or by default, will define your career for the next decade.

The first path is the deep specialist. These developers go further into technical depth than AI can follow. They work on problems that require genuine innovation. Novel algorithms, performance optimization at the hardware level, security research, compiler design, foundational AI and ML work. Their value comes from operating at the frontier of what is technically possible, in domains where AI tools are consumers of their work rather than competitors.

This is a valid and important path. But it is narrow. It requires exceptional talent in a specific domain, and the number of roles that genuinely need this level of specialization is smaller than most developers assume.

The second path is the AI operator. These developers become experts at leveraging AI tools to maximize their output. They master prompt engineering, learn to chain AI capabilities together, build workflows that multiply their productivity. They can produce the work of what used to take a small team.

This path is accessible and immediately rewarding. But it has a ceiling. As AI tools improve, the skill of operating them gets easier. Today's power user becomes tomorrow's baseline. The operator path is a strong short-term play, but it is a treadmill. You have to keep running just to stay in place.

The third path is the technical leader. These developers shift their focus from producing code to making decisions about what gets built and why. They translate between business needs and technical possibilities. They align teams. They manage complexity at the organizational level, not the code level. They still understand technology deeply, but they apply that understanding to strategy, communication, and leadership rather than implementation.

This is the path this book is about.

Not every developer should become a leader. Not every developer wants to. But if you have felt the ceiling of individual contribution, if you have sensed that your impact is constrained not by your coding ability but by your ability to influence, communicate, and align people, then this path is worth examining seriously.

Most developers will not make a conscious choice among these three paths. They will drift into one by default, usually the operator path, because it is the most natural extension of what they already do. Default choices have a way of becoming permanent ones. By the time you realize you have been on a treadmill, the developers who chose deliberately are already operating at a different altitude.

The Opportunity Hidden in the Shift

It is easy to read everything above as a threat narrative. AI is eating your job. Your core skill is commoditizing. The ground is shifting under your feet.

That reading is understandable. But it misses the larger picture.

For the first time in the history of software development, the barrier between technical understanding and organizational influence is dropping. Developers used to be locked in a box. You could build anything, but you had limited say in what got built or why. The division was clear. Business people decided. Developers executed. Your leverage was your ability to write code, and that leverage kept you in the build phase of every project.

AI changes the equation. When code production is no longer the bottleneck, the people who understand technology become valuable for their judgment, not their output. You can participate in strategy conversations not because you will go build the thing afterward, but because you understand what is possible, what is risky, and what is being overlooked.

Your technical knowledge becomes a lens for decision-making. Not just a tool for implementation.

The developer who understands distributed systems and can also articulate a product strategy to a room of executives is extraordinarily rare right now. The engineer who can evaluate a vendor's technical claims and translate the implications into business risk for a CFO is operating at a level most organizations desperately need but cannot find. These are not hypothetical roles. They are gaps that exist today in almost every technology company.

This is not a reduction of the developer's role. It is an expansion. But only for those willing to build beyond the skills that got them here.

What to Do Monday Morning

You do not need a new job title, a promotion, or a career change to start moving up the Value Shift Curve. You need three mindset shifts and the willingness to act on them this week.

Mindset shift one: stop measuring your day in output. The next time you finish work, do not count the tickets you closed or the pull requests you merged. Instead, ask yourself: what decision did I improve today? What misunderstanding did I prevent? What alignment did I create? If the answer is nothing, your day was productive but not valuable. Start tracking a different metric.

Mindset shift two: treat every meeting as a leadership opportunity. Most developers sit through product meetings, sprint planning, and stakeholder reviews as passive participants. They wait for someone to assign them work. This week, go in with a different posture. Ask a question about why a feature is prioritized the way it is. Raise a risk that nobody has mentioned. Offer a simpler alternative to a complex plan. Do not wait to be asked. The developers who get noticed as leadership material are the ones who contribute before the work is defined, not just after.

Mindset shift three: learn one thing about the business that has nothing to do with code. Find out how your company makes money. Understand the sales cycle. Read the last quarterly earnings call or board update if you have access. Talk to someone in customer success about the top three complaints. Technical leaders do not just understand systems. They understand the system the system exists inside. And most developers have never looked.

These are not career-changing moves in isolation. They are signals. They change how you think, what you notice, and what you bring to conversations. Over time, they shift your position on the curve.

Checklist: Are You Still Competing on Code?

Before moving to the next chapter, run through this honestly. These are not trick questions. There are no wrong answers. But they will tell you where you are on the Value Shift Curve and how urgently you need to move.

Do you measure your productivity primarily by code output, tickets closed, or features shipped? If yes, you are optimizing for a metric that is deflating.

Could a motivated mid-level developer with strong AI tools produce 80 percent of your weekly output? If the answer is even "maybe," your seniority premium is at risk.

When was the last time you influenced a product decision before it became a ticket? If you cannot remember, you are operating below your potential impact.

Do you understand why your team's current priorities are what they are? Not the technical what but the business why? If not, you are executing without context.

Have you ever presented a technical trade-off to a non-technical stakeholder and changed their decision? If not, your judgment is not reaching the people who set direction.

Could your manager articulate your value beyond "strong engineer, ships reliably"? If they cannot, you have a positioning problem that no amount of code will fix.

Do you know the names and priorities of the three most important stakeholders for your team's work? If not, you are building in a vacuum.

If more than half of these made you uncomfortable, good. Discomfort is the signal that there is room to grow. And the gap between where you are and where you could be is smaller than you think.

The next chapter digs into what that transition actually looks like. How to move from executing tasks to thinking strategically. And why that shift is harder than most developers expect.

CHAPTER 2

From Executor to Strategist

The Execution Trap

The promotion went to someone else.

You found out on a Thursday morning, in a meeting that was supposed to be about team restructuring. Your manager mentioned the new staff engineer role, and it was not your name. It was someone with fewer years at the company, a smaller commit history, and, if you were being honest, less raw technical ability than you.

After the meeting you went back to your desk and stared at your screen. You opened your git log almost reflexively, scrolling through months of commits. Feature after feature. Bug fixes. Performance optimizations. That migration everyone else was afraid to touch. You had shipped more code than anyone on the team in the last year. By any objective measure you could think of, you had outperformed the person who got the role.

Then you looked at what that person had actually done in the last six months. They had led the architecture review that aligned three teams on a shared platform strategy. They had written the technical vision document that the VP of Engineering kept referencing in all-hands meetings. They had spent weeks in conversations with product leadership, reshaping the roadmap to avoid a technical dead end that nobody else had flagged. They had not shipped as much code as you. But the code they influenced other people to ship had changed the trajectory of the product.

You had been the best executor on the team. They had been the person who decided what was worth executing.

That is the trap. And most developers do not see it until it has already closed around them.

Why Execution Alone Stops Working

Every developer starts their career the same way. You get a ticket. You understand the requirements. You write the code. You ship it. You get another ticket. This is how the job works, and for good reason. Early in your career, execution is everything. It is how you prove competence. It is how you earn trust. It is how you learn how systems actually behave when real users touch them. The feedback loop is tight and rewarding. You build something, it works, people use it. You get better at building things, you get harder problems, you build those too.

The trap is not that execution is bad. The trap is that execution is so satisfying, so clearly measurable, and so consistently rewarded that it becomes the only lens through which you see your work.

Most developers spend five, ten, fifteen years getting better at execution. They learn new languages, adopt new frameworks, optimize their workflows. They become the person on the team who can pick up any ticket and deliver it. They become reliable. Indispensable, even.

And then the rewards stop scaling.

You are doing more complex work than ever. You are solving harder problems than anyone around you. But the promotions slow down. The recognition flattens. New developers join the team and ship features almost as fast as you do, sometimes with AI tools doing half the work.

Here is where execution fails as a strategy. Execution is linear. You do one thing, then the next, then the next. Your output is bounded by your time, your energy, and your attention. You can get faster. You can get more efficient. But you are still one person doing one thing at a time. The ceiling is built into the model.

The developers who break through that ceiling are not faster executors. They are people who changed what they were executing on. They stopped optimizing for throughput and started optimizing for direction. They realized that doing the right thing at half speed creates more value than doing the wrong thing at full speed.

This is where most developers feel stuck. They assume the problem is that they need to get even better at execution. Learn another framework. Ship faster. Take on more tickets.

The real problem is that execution was never going to take them where they want to go.

The 4-Level Impact Model

There is a way to make this shift concrete. Think about developer impact as operating at four distinct levels, each one further from the ticket queue and closer to the outcomes that actually move the business.

Level one is Tasks. This is where everyone starts. You receive a well-defined unit of work, you complete it, and you move on. Your impact is measured by the quality and speed of your output. At this level, the thinking has been done for you. Your job is to translate decisions into working software. There is nothing wrong with this level. But the ceiling is low, and with AI tools now handling much of what used to require experience, it is getting lower.

Level two is Features. At this level, you are not just completing tasks. You are owning entire features from design through delivery. You make decisions about implementation approach, you coordinate with other team members, you handle the complexity of integrating your work into a larger system. Your scope is broader. Your judgment matters more. But you are still operating within someone else's definition of what needs to be built. The feature was defined upstream. You own the how, but not the what or the why.

Level three is Systems. This is where the shift starts to matter. At the systems level, you are thinking about how components interact, how teams depend on each other, how technical decisions create downstream consequences that nobody scoped. You see the architecture not as a diagram on a wiki page but as a living set of constraints that shape what the organization can and cannot do. You start influencing decisions that affect multiple teams, multiple quarters, and multiple outcomes simultaneously. The questions you ask at this level are different. Not "how do I build this feature?" but "how does this feature affect the reliability of the platform?" and "what technical debt are we creating that nobody is tracking?"

Level four is Outcomes. This is the level where technical knowledge meets strategic impact. At the outcomes level, you are not thinking about what to build. You are thinking about what the business needs to achieve and working backward to the technical decisions that enable it. You evaluate features not by their engineering elegance but by whether they drive the metrics that matter. You kill projects that are technically impressive but strategically irrelevant. You redirect effort toward the highest-leverage work, even when it is less interesting from a pure engineering perspective.

Most developers operate between levels one and two for their entire careers. The ones who get promoted to staff and principal roles operate consistently at level three. The ones who end up as VPs of Engineering and CTOs operate at level four. And the gap between each level is not about being smarter or working harder. It is about changing what you pay attention to.

Ask yourself an honest question. When was the last time your work created impact at level three or four? If you cannot point to a specific example, you now know where the gap is.

Two Engineers, One Feature, Opposite Outcomes

A product manager at a B2B SaaS company writes a spec for an advanced analytics dashboard. The spec is detailed. Wireframes, user stories, acceptance criteria. Two senior engineers on different teams are each assigned a major component of the build.

The first engineer, call him Marcus, does exactly what strong engineers do. He breaks the spec into tasks, estimates the work, and starts building. He designs a flexible schema for custom metrics. He builds a real-time aggregation pipeline that can handle the query patterns the wireframes imply. He writes tests. He optimizes query performance until the dashboard loads in under two seconds. The code is clean. The architecture is extensible. He delivers on time, slightly under budget. His tech lead calls it one of the best implementations the team has shipped.

Six months later, the dashboard is used by fewer than eight percent of the customer base. Usage data shows that most customers open it once, maybe twice, then never return. The metrics the dashboard surfaces do not map to the decisions customers actually need to make. The real-time updates that Marcus optimized are irrelevant because the customers who do use it check it once a week at most. The feature becomes maintenance burden. Nobody wants to own it. In the next planning cycle, the product team quietly deprioritizes it.

Marcus built a technically excellent product that solved a problem nobody actually had.

The second engineer, call her Priya, took the same spec and did something different before she wrote a single line of code. She pulled the support ticket data for the top twenty enterprise accounts. She noticed that the most common analytics-related request was not “show me a dashboard” but “help me prove ROI to my CFO.” She set up three calls with customers who had asked for better analytics. On every call, the same pattern emerged. They did not want a dashboard. They wanted a report they could export and hand to their finance team. Something with clear numbers, clean formatting, and a narrative that tied usage metrics to business outcomes.

Priya went back to the product manager with a proposal. Instead of the full dashboard, build a monthly ROI report generator. Half the engineering effort. A fraction of the ongoing maintenance. And it directly addressed the problem customers were actually trying to solve. The product manager pushed back at first. The dashboard was already in the roadmap. Leadership had signed off on it. But Priya brought the customer data, the support ticket analysis, and a prototype that took her two days. The product manager took it to the VP of Product, who approved the pivot.

The ROI report launched two months later. Within a quarter, it was used by sixty percent of enterprise accounts. The customer success team reported that it became one of their top tools for renewal conversations. Net retention for accounts using the report was twelve points higher than for those that did not.

Priya shipped less code than Marcus. She wrote a simpler system. By every traditional engineering metric, her contribution was smaller. But her impact was ten times larger because she operated at level four of the Impact Model. She traced the feature back to the outcome the business actually needed and built for that instead.

Same starting point. Same spec. One engineer executed. The other one questioned. The gap between those two approaches is the gap between a productive career and an impactful one.

What Most Developers Get Wrong About Strategy

The word “strategy” makes most developers uncomfortable. It sounds like something that happens in conference rooms with whiteboards and sticky notes, led by people with MBA degrees who do not understand how systems actually work. It sounds political. It sounds soft.

That reaction is understandable and wrong.

Strategy, for a developer, is not about creating slide decks or using business jargon. It is about understanding why things are being built and whether the reasons hold up to scrutiny. It is about having an opinion, grounded in technical reality, about what the team should be doing differently. It is about making decisions that compound rather than decisions that expire.

Here are three things most developers get wrong about strategy.

The first is thinking strategy is someone else's job. In most organizations, the product manager defines the roadmap, the engineering manager allocates capacity, and the developer executes. That division of labor is real. But it is not a law of physics. It is a default that exists because most developers never challenged it. The product manager does not have a monopoly on good ideas about what to build. They have context you do not. And you have context they do not. The developer who understands the technical constraints, the system's actual behavior under load, the architectural debt that is silently shaping what is possible, has strategic information that nobody else in the room possesses. Keeping it to yourself is not humility. It is a failure to add the value you are uniquely positioned to add.

The second is confusing strategy with planning. Planning is about sequencing work. Strategy is about choosing what work matters. You can have an impeccable plan for building the wrong thing. You can have a flawless sprint cadence, detailed story points, and a burndown chart that would make a project manager weep with joy, and still waste three months on a feature that never should have existed. Planning is necessary. Strategy is what makes planning worthwhile.

The third is believing strategy requires certainty. Developers are trained to value precision. When the requirements are ambiguous, the instinct is to ask for clarification. When the direction is unclear, the instinct is to wait. This is exactly the wrong posture for strategic thinking. Strategy happens in the space of uncertainty. It is about making the best decision you can with incomplete information, then adjusting as you learn. The developer who waits for perfect clarity before forming an opinion will always be behind the developer who forms a thoughtful opinion early and updates it as evidence arrives.

Strategy is not a personality trait. It is a practice. And like any practice, it starts with small, deliberate actions that compound over time.

The Shift from Execution to Strategy

The difference between an executor and a strategist is not intelligence or experience. It is orientation.

Executors look at a problem and ask, "How do we build this?" They are focused on implementation. They think about architecture, patterns, timelines, and delivery. These are important questions, and good executors are valuable.

Strategists look at the same problem and ask a different question first. "Should we build this at all?"

That single question changes the entire conversation. It forces you to think about the problem behind the request. It makes you evaluate whether the proposed solution is the best use of the team's time. It shifts your focus from delivery to impact.

Most developers never ask that question. Not because they do not care, but because the organizational structure does not encourage it. The product manager wrote the spec. The designer made the mockups. The engineering manager put it in the sprint. By the time it reaches the developer, it feels like the thinking has already been done.

But here is what actually happens in most organizations. Product managers are overloaded. They are juggling stakeholders, timelines, and competing priorities. Their specs often reflect the loudest request, not the most important one. Designers work from the same imperfect inputs. Engineering managers are balancing capacity, not evaluating strategy.

Nobody in the chain has the full picture. And the developer, who actually understands the technical constraints, dependencies, and system-level implications, is the one person who could add the most clarity. But they do not, because they were trained to execute, not to question.

The strategist breaks this pattern. They do not reject the work. They enrich it. They bring technical perspective to strategic conversations. They surface trade-offs that nobody else can see. They make the team's decisions better by contributing their understanding of what is actually possible, what is risky, and what is being overlooked.

Execution without strategy is motion without direction. Strategy without execution is ideas without impact. The developers who do both are the ones organizations cannot afford to lose.

Where Careers Slow Down

There is a moment in most developers' careers that feels like hitting a wall. It usually happens around the senior engineer level. You have the technical skills. You have the experience. You have earned respect from your peers. And yet the path forward becomes unclear.

The reason is structural. Most engineering organizations have a narrow top. There are many junior and mid-level roles, fewer senior roles, and very few principal or staff-level positions. The higher you go, the less the job is about writing code and the more it is about something else entirely.

That something else is what most developers never trained for.

At the senior level, the people who keep advancing are not the ones who write the best code. They are the ones who make the best decisions. They see patterns across teams, not just within their own codebase. They understand the business context behind technical choices. They communicate clearly to people who do not write code. They influence direction without needing to be in charge.

The developers who stay stuck at the senior level are often technically stronger than the people who move past them. They can debug faster, architect more elegantly, and ship more reliably. But they operate within the boundaries of what is asked of them. They execute brilliantly inside a box that someone else designed.

This is where careers plateau. Not because of a lack of skill, but because of a mismatch between the skill being optimized and the skill being valued.

The transition from senior engineer to technical leader is not a promotion. It is a transformation in how you think about your role. You stop measuring yourself by the quality of your code and start measuring yourself by the quality of your decisions. You stop asking how to build things and start asking what should be built and why.

That sounds simple. In practice, it is one of the hardest shifts a developer will ever make.

Thinking in Outcomes Instead of Tasks

One of the most common traps in software development is confusing activity with progress. You can close fifty tickets in a sprint and still not move the needle on anything that matters.

Tasks hide the real goal. They are fragments of a plan that someone translated into actionable units. By the time you are reading a Jira ticket, the original intent has been filtered, compressed, and sometimes distorted. The ticket says "add a CSV export button." The actual goal was "help enterprise customers get their data into internal reporting tools." Those are not the same thing. One is a task. The other is an outcome.

When you think in tasks, you optimize for completion. Did the button get shipped? Does it work? Great. Move on.

When you think in outcomes, you optimize for impact. Will enterprise customers actually use this? Is CSV the right format, or do most of them need an API integration? Are we solving the export problem, or are we solving the retention problem that the export problem is a symptom of?

This is not about overcomplicating things. It is about understanding what you are actually trying to accomplish before you start building. The developer who asks "what outcome are we trying to drive?" before writing a line of code will consistently make better decisions than the developer who asks "what are the acceptance criteria?"

Here is a practical example. A product manager asks the team to build a notification system so users know when their reports are ready. The task-oriented developer starts designing the notification architecture. Push notifications, email, in-app alerts, queueing systems. The outcome-oriented developer asks a different question. Why do users need to be notified? Is the report taking too long? Would it be better to make the report faster so there is nothing to wait for?

Same request. Completely different approach. The second developer might eliminate the need for the feature entirely, saving weeks of work and delivering a better user experience. That is the power of thinking in outcomes.

The shift is simple to describe and difficult to practice. It requires you to resist the pull of implementation, which is where most developers feel most comfortable, and stay in the problem space longer. It means sitting with ambiguity instead of rushing to a solution. It means asking questions that might make you look like you do not understand the task, when in reality, you understand it more deeply than anyone else in the room.

Expanding Influence

There is a common misconception that influence requires authority. That you need a title, a team, or a mandate before you can shape direction.

That is backwards. In most organizations, the people with the most influence earned it long before they had the title to match. They earned it by being right often enough that people started listening. By being clear enough that people started quoting them. By being consistent enough that people started trusting their judgment.

For developers, influence starts in three areas.

The first is architecture. Every architectural decision shapes what the team can and cannot do for months or years. The developer who can articulate why a particular approach is better, not just technically but in terms of business impact, maintenance cost, and team velocity, has enormous influence over the direction of the product. This does not require being the most senior person in the room. It requires being the clearest thinker in the room.

The second is product decisions. Most developers wait to be told what to build. The ones who grow fastest are the ones who bring ideas to the table. They notice patterns in support tickets that suggest a deeper problem. They see data that contradicts the product roadmap. They propose alternatives that save time or improve outcomes. They earn a seat at the product table not by demanding it but by consistently adding value to the conversation.

The third is team direction. This is not about management. It is about shaping how the team works. The developer who introduces better processes, who mentors junior engineers effectively, who identifies bottlenecks and proposes solutions, is leading without a title. They are making the team better, and everyone notices.

Influence grows in layers. First your team trusts your technical judgment. Then they trust your product judgment. Then people outside your team start seeking your input. Then leadership starts including you in decisions you were never part of before.

None of this requires permission. It requires showing up with clarity, context, and good judgment consistently enough that people start relying on it.

That is how careers accelerate. Not through promotions. Through demonstrated influence that makes the promotion inevitable.

The Strategic Developer Framework

If strategy feels abstract, it helps to have a concrete tool. Before building anything significant, ask four questions. Write them down. Discuss them with your team. Do not skip them.

The first question is: what problem are we actually solving?

Not what feature are we building. Not what ticket are we working on. What is the underlying problem that prompted this work? This question sounds obvious, but the answer is often surprising. Teams regularly build solutions to symptoms rather than root causes. The developer who can trace a feature request back to the real problem it is trying to address will consistently make better decisions about how to solve it, or whether to solve it at all.

The second question is: what outcome matters most?

Every project has multiple possible outcomes. Speed to market. User satisfaction. System reliability. Revenue impact. They all matter, but they cannot all be the top priority. Knowing which outcome the organization values most for this particular effort changes how you approach it. Optimizing for speed looks very different from optimizing for reliability. The strategist knows which one matters before they write the first line of code.

The third question is: what trade-offs are we accepting?

Every technical decision involves trade-offs. Speed versus quality. Flexibility versus simplicity. Short-term velocity versus long-term maintainability. Most teams make these trade-offs implicitly, without discussion. The strategic developer makes them explicit. They name the trade-off out loud. They make sure the team and the stakeholders understand what is being gained and what is being given up. This is not about being cautious. It is about being honest. And it builds enormous trust.

The fourth question is: what does success look like six months from now?

This is the question that separates task thinking from outcome thinking. If you ship the feature and walk away, you are an executor. If you define what success looks like after the feature has been in production for six months, you are a strategist. This question forces you to think about adoption, maintenance, iteration, and long-term impact. It connects your work today to the results that actually matter to the business.

These four questions are not a checklist. They are a thinking discipline. You will not always have perfect answers. Sometimes you will surface more ambiguity than clarity. That is fine. The act of asking them changes how you approach your work. It moves you from reacting to requests to shaping them. From building what is asked for to building what is needed.

That is the shift. And it compounds over time.

What to Do Monday Morning

You do not need to reinvent yourself to start operating strategically. You need two habits, practiced consistently, starting this week.

Habit one: ask better questions in meetings. Most developers sit in sprint planning, product reviews, and roadmap discussions as receivers. They take in information, process it, and wait for the work to arrive. This week, change your posture. In the next meeting where work is being discussed, ask one of these questions. Why is this the most important thing we could be working on right now? What happens if we do not build this? Who are we building this for, and have we talked to them? How will we know this was successful?

You do not have to ask all of them. Pick one. Ask it genuinely, not as a challenge but as a contribution. The first time, people will be surprised. The third time, they will start expecting it. By the tenth time, you will be part of the conversation before it gets to the ticket queue.

Habit two: reframe one task into an outcome. Look at the next ticket you pick up. Before you start building, write one sentence that describes the outcome this task is meant to produce. Not "implement the API endpoint." Something like "enable partners to pull their transaction data without contacting support, reducing support ticket volume by an estimated 30 percent." If you cannot write that sentence, you do not have enough context to build the right thing. Go get the context. Ask the product manager. Check the analytics. Read the support tickets.

This takes fifteen minutes. It changes how you approach the work. Over time, it changes how the team approaches the work, because you start asking the question out loud and other people start doing it too.

Small actions, practiced consistently, compound into a different way of working. And a different way of working leads to a different career trajectory.

Checklist: Are You Operating as an Executor or a Strategist?

Before moving to the next chapter, run through this honestly. No judgment. Just positioning.

When you pick up a new task, do you start by understanding the acceptance criteria or by understanding the business problem behind it? If criteria, you are operating at level one or two of the Impact Model.

In the last month, have you questioned whether a planned feature was the right approach to the underlying problem? If not, you are executing someone else's strategy without contributing your own perspective.

Can you describe, in one sentence, the business outcome your current project is meant to drive? If not, you are building without a compass.

When your team makes a technical decision, do you evaluate it in terms of code quality or in terms of business impact? If the former, your strategic muscle is underdeveloped.

Have you ever killed, redirected, or significantly reshaped a project based on your own analysis? If yes, you are already operating strategically. If not, you may be deferring judgment you are qualified to exercise.

Do you know the top three priorities of your product team and how your engineering work connects to them? If not, you are executing in a vacuum.

When was the last time someone outside your engineering team sought your input on a business or product decision? If it has been more than two months, your influence radius is smaller than your capability.

Could your manager describe your impact beyond "ships reliably and writes good code"? If not, you have a positioning problem that no amount of technical excellence will solve.

If more than half of these pointed toward executor, that is not a failure. It is a starting position. The gap between executing well and thinking strategically is smaller than most developers believe. It starts with one question, asked in one meeting, followed through with genuine curiosity. That is the entire beginning.

The next chapter explores the specific skill that separates developers who influence decisions from those who wait for them: communication that moves people without writing code.

CHAPTER 3

Communication That Moves Code Without Writing It

Trained to Talk to Machines

Developers spend years learning to communicate with extraordinary precision. Every semicolon matters. Every variable name carries meaning. Every function signature is a contract. The machine does exactly what you tell it to do, no more and no less, and when something goes wrong the fault is always traceable to something you said incorrectly.

This is a powerful training. It builds a mind that values clarity, specificity, and logical structure. It teaches you to think in systems and express yourself without ambiguity.

It also ruins you for talking to humans.

Human communication does not work like code. People do not parse your words literally. They filter everything through context, emotion, politics, prior experience, and their own priorities. A perfectly logical argument can fail completely if it is delivered at the wrong time, to the wrong audience, or in the wrong tone. A technically correct explanation can confuse everyone in the room if it is pitched at the wrong level of abstraction.

Most developers know this intellectually. Very few have internalized it as a skill to practice. They spend hundreds of hours improving their code quality and almost none improving how they communicate ideas to the people who decide what gets built, funded, and prioritized.

This is one of the highest-leverage gaps in most developers' careers. Not because communication is more important than technical skill, but because it is the multiplier that determines how far your technical skill can reach.

The best idea in the room is worthless if nobody understands it. The best technical analysis is wasted if it never leaves the engineer's head. The most important architectural concern is invisible if it cannot be translated into language that a product manager, a designer, or an executive can act on.

Communication is not a soft skill. That label has done more damage to engineering careers than any technology shift. It frames communication as something peripheral, something you either have a knack for or you do not, something nice to have after the real work is done. That framing is wrong. Communication is a technical skill. It has inputs, outputs, failure modes, and optimization strategies. It can be measured by whether it produces the intended result. And like any technical skill, it improves with deliberate practice and degrades with neglect.

Communication is the mechanism through which technical judgment becomes organizational impact.

The Translation Layer

If you have spent any time building distributed systems, you understand the concept of a translation layer. It sits between two components that speak different protocols, converting messages from one format into another so they can interoperate without either side needing to understand the other's internal representation.

Your communication needs the same architecture.

Think of it as three layers, each translating the same reality into a different protocol.

Layer one is Code. This is the language you speak with other engineers. It is precise, technical, and assumes shared context. When you say "we need to denormalize the read path and add a caching layer," another engineer knows exactly what you mean. They understand the trade-offs, the implementation implications, and the system behavior that motivates the change. This layer is where most developers live. It is comfortable. It is efficient. And it is completely opaque to anyone outside engineering.

Layer two is System. This is where you translate code-level reality into operational language that your cross-functional team can use. Product managers, designers, QA leads, and project managers operate at this level. They do not need to know about denormalization. They need to know that the page loads slowly for customers with large accounts, that the fix requires two sprints of work, and that it will also enable a feature they have been requesting for months. At this layer, you are not simplifying. You are converting technical facts into operational decisions. The system layer answers questions like: what does this mean for the timeline? What is the user impact? What are the risks?

Layer three is Business Outcome. This is where you speak to directors, VPs, and executives. They are allocating resources across the entire organization. They do not care about page load times unless those times connect to revenue, retention, or competitive positioning. At this layer, the same database change becomes: "Enterprise customers on our largest tier are reporting performance issues that correlate with a 15 percent increase in support tickets and a measurable dip in NPS. The fix addresses the root cause, reduces support load, and unblocks the analytics feature that three of our top ten accounts have been requesting." Same reality. Different protocol. Maximum signal for the audience receiving it.

The Translation Layer is not about dumbing things down. That framing is part of why developers resist doing it. Nobody wants to feel like they are simplifying their expertise for people who do not understand it. The real reframe is this: translation is about increasing the resolution of your communication, not decreasing it. When you explain a database migration to another engineer, you use technical terms because they carry a lot of information efficiently. When you explain the same migration to a VP of Product, different terms carry more information. "This requires two weeks of engineering time and the feature will be unavailable to customers for four hours" is higher resolution for that audience than any discussion of schema changes and rollback strategies.

The mistake most developers make is thinking that their technical explanation is the complete version and everything else is a simplification. In reality, every audience needs a different complete version. The engineering version is complete for engineers. The business version is complete for executives. Neither is a dumbed-down copy of the other. They are different lenses on the same underlying reality, optimized for different decision-making contexts.

The developers who master the Translation Layer do not just get heard. They get consulted. They become the person that product managers pull into roadmap discussions, that executives invite to strategy reviews, that other teams call when they need someone who can bridge the gap between what the system does and what the business needs.

Right Solution, Wrong Room

Here is a story that plays out in organizations every week.

A senior backend engineer named Daniel has been tracking a growing problem. The company's notification system was built three years ago as a monolith. It handles email, push, SMS, and in-app alerts through a single service. As the user base has grown, the system has become a bottleneck. Delivery latency is climbing. The queue backs up during peak hours. Every new notification type requires changes to a shared codebase that four teams depend on, creating merge conflicts and deployment risks.

Daniel has the right solution. He has designed an event-driven architecture that decouples notification channels into independent services. Each channel scales independently. Teams can deploy without coordinating. The system can handle ten times the current load. He has benchmarked it. He has prototyped the critical path. He is confident.

The product leadership team schedules a meeting to discuss the notification reliability problems that customers have been escalating. Daniel is invited. He prepares a detailed technical presentation. Twelve slides. Architecture diagrams. Performance benchmarks. Migration plan with phases and rollback strategies.

He walks through the presentation methodically. He explains the current architecture's limitations. He describes the event-driven alternative. He shows the benchmarks. He answers technical questions from the other engineers in the room.

The VP of Product listens politely, then asks one question. "What is the customer impact if we do nothing for the next quarter?"

Daniel pauses. He talks about queue depth and P99 latency. He mentions the deployment coupling problem. He references a recent incident where a bad deploy to the notification service took down alerts for two hours.

The VP nods and turns to the product manager. "Is this affecting retention?" The product manager says the data is unclear. A few enterprise accounts have complained, but churn has not spiked. The VP says they will revisit it next quarter and moves on to the next topic. The meeting ends. Daniel's proposal is shelved.

Here is what Daniel got wrong. His solution was technically correct. His analysis was thorough. His architecture was sound. But he communicated at layer one, Code, in a room that was operating at layer three, Business Outcome. He described system behavior when the room needed to hear business impact. He presented benchmarks when the VP needed to understand revenue risk. He answered the wrong question with the right data.

The VP was not asking about P99 latency. The VP was asking: should I allocate engineering resources to this problem instead of the three other problems competing for the same team's time? That is a business question. It requires a business answer. And Daniel never provided one.

His proposal did not fail because it was wrong. It failed because it was never translated.

Same Problem, Different Engineer

Now imagine the same meeting, but a different engineer presents.

Nadia has been tracking the same notification issues Daniel identified. She has the same technical understanding. She has seen the same queue backups and deployment risks. But before the meeting, she does something Daniel did not. She talks to the customer success team and pulls the data on notification-related support tickets over the last six months. She talks to the sales team and learns that two enterprise prospects specifically asked about notification reliability during their evaluations. She checks the product analytics and finds that users who experience delayed notifications have a 23 percent lower 30-day retention rate than users who do not.

In the meeting, Nadia does not open with architecture diagrams. She opens with this: "Notification delays are costing us customers. Users who experience late notifications retain at 23 percent below average. We have had two enterprise prospects flag reliability concerns during sales calls. Support tickets related to notifications have tripled in six months. The root cause is architectural, and I have a fix that addresses it, but the reason we should prioritize it is that this is now a revenue problem, not just an engineering problem."

The VP leans forward. "What does the fix look like in terms of timeline and risk?"

Nadia answers at layer two. "Two sprints for the core migration. We can phase it so email, which is the highest-volume channel, moves first. Customers see improvement within three weeks. The rest follows over the next quarter. Risk is low because each channel migrates independently, so we can roll back any single channel without affecting the others."

The VP turns to the product manager. "Let's reprioritize. Can we fit this into the next cycle?"

Same problem. Same solution. Different outcome. The difference was not technical skill. It was communication architecture. Nadia operated across all three layers of the Translation Layer. She started at Business Outcome, moved to System when asked for details, and kept Code in reserve for the engineers who would need it during implementation. She did not present information. She structured a decision.

That is what communication as a technical skill looks like. It has a clear input (the audience's decision-making context), a defined process (translating through the appropriate layer), and a measurable output (the decision was made, the resources were allocated, the work got prioritized). There is nothing soft about it.

Why Engineers Struggle in Meetings

Meetings are where decisions get made. And if you are not in the room when the decision happens, or if you are in the room but not contributing effectively, then your technical judgment does not factor into the outcome. This is not a theory. This is how organizations operate.

The problem is not that engineers are bad at meetings. The problem is that meetings operate on a protocol that engineers were never trained for.

In code, precision is rewarded. The more specific and complete your expression, the better the outcome. In meetings, precision often backfires. A technically complete answer to a question nobody was really asking burns two minutes of airtime and moves the room nowhere. The signal gets lost in the noise of detail.

In code, the best argument wins. Logic is the arbiter. In meetings, the clearest argument wins, which is not always the same thing. A less optimal idea, expressed clearly and connected to what the room cares about, will beat a superior idea that is expressed in language the room cannot parse.

In code, sequence matters. You build from foundations up. In meetings, the bottom-up approach kills you. By the time you have laid the groundwork for your point, someone else has spoken, the conversation has moved on, and your window has closed. Meetings reward people who lead with the conclusion and support it on demand.

In code, completeness is a virtue. You handle every edge case. In meetings, completeness is the enemy. Nobody needs your edge cases. They need your recommendation, the top two reasons behind it, and your answer to the obvious objection. Everything else is available if asked.

These are not personality differences. They are protocol mismatches. An engineer who understands these mismatches can adapt their communication the same way they would adapt their code to a different runtime environment. The logic is the same. The interface changes.

There is one more reason engineers struggle in meetings that nobody talks about. Fear of being wrong. Engineers are trained in environments where being wrong has immediate, visible consequences. The test fails. The build breaks. The bug ships. This trains a deep aversion to stating things you are not certain about. In meetings, this manifests as silence. The engineer has a strong intuition about the right direction but will not voice it because they have not fully validated it yet. Meanwhile, the product manager with 60 percent confidence states their position clearly and the room moves in that direction.

Being approximately right in a meeting is more valuable than being precisely right after the meeting. The engineer who says “I am not certain, but my instinct is that approach B has a significant scaling risk we should investigate before committing” has contributed more than the engineer who stays silent, validates the concern at their desk afterward, and mentions it in a Slack message two days later when the decision has already been made.

What Most Developers Get Wrong About Communication

Three misconceptions keep engineers from developing communication as a real skill.

The first is treating communication as self-expression. Most developers, when they communicate, are trying to express what they know. They are transmitting information from their head into the room. This is the wrong mental model. Effective communication is not about what you want to say. It is about what the listener needs to hear in order to make a better decision. These are fundamentally different orientations. One is speaker-centered. The other is audience-centered. The developer who asks "what do I need to explain?" will always be less effective than the developer who asks "what does this person need to understand in order to act?"

The second is believing that good ideas sell themselves. They do not. Good ideas, poorly communicated, lose to mediocre ideas that are well-framed. This is not a flaw in the system. It is a feature. Organizations cannot evaluate ideas in their raw technical form. They evaluate ideas as they are presented, which means the presentation is part of the idea. The developer who says "the work should speak for itself" is opting out of a game that everyone else is playing. The work does not speak for itself. You speak for the work. And how well you do that determines whether the work matters.

The third is confusing frequency with effectiveness. Some developers try to improve their communication by talking more. They volunteer opinions in every meeting. They write longer emails. They send more Slack messages. This is counterproductive. Communication effectiveness is not about volume. It is about signal density. The developer who speaks three times in a meeting but each statement reframes the conversation or surfaces a critical trade-off has more communication impact than the developer who speaks fifteen times with incremental technical observations. Less, sharper, better-timed. That is the formula.

There is a diagnostic that cuts through all three misconceptions. After your next meeting, ask yourself: did anything I said change a decision, clarify a disagreement, or move the conversation toward resolution? If the answer is no, your communication was noise, regardless of how technically accurate it was.

The Force Multiplier

Think about the developers you have worked with who had outsized influence. Not the ones with the most impressive GitHub profiles or the deepest framework knowledge. The ones who actually shaped what the team built and how it operated.

Almost without exception, they were strong communicators.

They could explain a complex system in terms anyone could follow. They could walk into a meeting, cut through thirty minutes of confusion with a single clear statement, and realign the entire room. They could write a design document that made the right approach feel obvious. They could deliver bad news without creating panic and push back on a bad idea without creating enemies.

These are not personality traits. They are skills. And they function as a force multiplier on everything else a developer can do.

Here is how the math works. A developer who can solve hard problems but cannot communicate their thinking has an impact radius of one. They do excellent work, but it stops at the boundary of what they personally touch. A developer with the same technical ability who can also communicate effectively has an impact radius that extends across the entire team, and sometimes across the entire organization. They shape decisions they are not directly involved in. They prevent mistakes before they happen. They accelerate the work of everyone around them.

The gap between these two developers is not talent. It is communication. And it compounds over time. The developer who communicates well gets included in more conversations, which gives them more context, which makes their contributions more valuable, which gets them included in even more conversations. The developer who does not stays in their lane, doing good work that nobody outside the team fully appreciates.

This is not fair. But it is how organizations work. And once you see the pattern, you cannot unsee it. The developers who advance fastest are not always the most technically gifted. They are the ones who can make their technical gifts visible and useful to the people making decisions.

The good news is that communication is a learnable skill. You do not need to be charismatic. You do not need to be an extrovert. You need to be clear, deliberate, and willing to practice. The same discipline that made you a good developer can make you a good communicator. It just requires turning that discipline toward a different kind of problem.

Meetings as Decision Engines

Developers hate meetings. This is one of the most universal sentiments in the industry and it is largely justified. Most meetings are poorly run, lack clear purpose, and could have been an email.

But here is what most developers miss. Meetings are where decisions get made. And if you treat meetings as something to endure rather than something to use, you are surrendering your influence at the exact moment it matters most.

A strategically minded developer treats every meeting as a decision engine. Before the meeting, they ask: what decision is being made here? If there is no clear decision, they question whether the meeting should happen at all. During the meeting, they listen for the actual points of disagreement rather than waiting for their turn to present a technical opinion. They intervene at the moment their technical perspective can resolve ambiguity or clarify a trade-off. After the meeting, they confirm what was decided and what the next steps are.

This sounds obvious. Almost nobody does it.

Most developers in meetings do one of two things. They stay quiet and leave frustrated that bad decisions were made without their input. Or they talk too much about technical details and leave frustrated that nobody listened.

The developers who use meetings effectively do something different. They wait for the moment when the conversation is stuck, when two sides are talking past each other, when an assumption is going unchallenged, or when a decision is about to be made without key information. Then they speak up with a clear, concise statement that moves the conversation forward.

“I think the real question here is whether we can afford the four-week timeline, because the alternative introduces a risk we have not discussed.”

That is one sentence. It reframes the conversation. It surfaces a trade-off. It moves the room toward a better decision. And it positions the developer who said it as someone whose judgment matters.

This is communication as a leadership tool. Not talking more. Not presenting more slides. Not sending longer emails. Speaking at the right moment, with the right framing, to the right audience. Every time you do this well, you earn more trust. Every time you earn more trust, you get invited into more of the conversations where the real decisions happen.

Writing That Creates Alignment

Not all communication happens in meetings. Some of the most impactful communication a developer can produce is written. Design documents, technical proposals, decision summaries, project retrospectives. These artifacts persist. They get shared. They get referenced weeks and months after they were written. They shape thinking even when you are not in the room.

Most developers write for themselves instead of for their audience. They produce documents that are technically thorough but organizationally useless. A twenty-page design document that nobody reads has zero impact. A one-page summary that every stakeholder reads and acts on has enormous impact.

The pattern is the same as verbal communication. Start with the problem. State the recommendation. Explain the trade-offs. Make it easy for the reader to understand what you are proposing and why, without requiring them to read every detail.

Put the most important information first. Not the background. Not the history. Not the technical context. The recommendation. If someone reads only the first paragraph, they should understand what you are proposing and what decision you need from them. Everything else supports that opening.

This is hard for developers because it feels backwards. You want to build the argument from the ground up, showing your work the way you would prove a theorem. But your reader is not a professor grading your proof. They are a busy person who needs to make a decision. Give them the answer first. Let them dig into the reasoning only if they want to.

The developers who write this way become disproportionately influential. Their documents get read. Their proposals get approved. Their framing becomes the default language the team uses to talk about problems. That is communication creating alignment at scale, long after the meeting is over and the Slack thread has been buried.

What to Do Monday Morning

You do not need to overhaul how you communicate. You need three specific changes, practiced consistently, starting this week.

The first change: lead with the so-what, not the how. In your next meeting, when you have something to contribute, resist the urge to explain the technical context first. Instead, start with what your point means for the decision being discussed. Instead of "The current API has a rate-limiting issue that causes 429 errors when batch processing exceeds 1,000 requests per minute," try "If we launch with the current API, large customers will hit errors within the first week. Here is why." The technical detail supports the statement. It does not lead it. Practice this inversion until it feels natural. It will not feel natural at first.

The second change: match your layer to the room. Before you speak, take one second to ask yourself: who is making the decision in this room, and what layer of the Translation Layer do they operate on? If it is engineers, speak Code. If it is product managers, speak System. If it is leadership, speak Business Outcome. You do not need to guess. You can listen for cues. Are they asking about implementation details? Speak Code. Are they asking about timelines and user impact? Speak System. Are they asking about revenue, risk, or strategic priority? Speak Business Outcome. The act of consciously choosing your layer before speaking will immediately improve how your contributions land.

The third change: prepare one decision-ready statement before every meeting. Look at the meeting agenda. Identify the core decision being discussed. Write one sentence that frames the most important trade-off or surfaces the information the room will need. Bring that sentence to the meeting. You may not use it. The conversation may go in a different direction. But having it prepared means that when the moment arrives, you are ready to contribute something that moves the room forward rather than scrambling for the right words while the window closes.

These are small, concrete adjustments. None of them require a personality change or a public speaking course. They require the same kind of deliberate practice you applied when you learned to write clean code. You were not born knowing how to name variables well or structure functions clearly. You practiced until the good patterns became automatic. Communication works the same way.

The Cost of Not Communicating

There is a hidden cost to poor communication that most developers never see. It is the decisions that get made without them.

Every day, product managers are prioritizing features based on incomplete technical understanding. Executives are allocating budgets based on risk assessments that no engineer reviewed. Design teams are proposing solutions that are technically expensive or impossible, and nobody catches it until development is underway.

These are not failures of malice or incompetence. They are failures of communication. The technical knowledge existed inside the engineering team. It just never reached the people who needed it, in a form they could use, at the moment the decision was being made.

The developer who communicates well prevents these failures. Not by attending every meeting or reviewing every decision, but by building a reputation as someone who translates technical reality into clear, actionable information. People start seeking them out. They get included earlier in the process. They catch problems before they become expensive.

The developer who does not communicate well never knows what they missed. They only see the symptoms. Bad requirements. Wrong priorities. Unrealistic timelines. They blame product. They blame management. They blame the process.

The real problem was that their expertise never left the IDE.

Checklist: Are You Communicating for Engineers or for Decisions?

Before moving to the next chapter, run through this honestly.

When you explain a technical problem, do you start with the implementation details or with the business impact? If you start with the details, you are communicating at Code layer in rooms that need System or Business Outcome layer.

In your last three meetings, did you adjust your language based on who was in the room? If you spoke the same way to engineers, product managers, and executives, you are using a single protocol for multiple audiences.

Can your product manager explain your current project's technical risks in their own words? If not, your translation is not landing. The test of communication is not what you said. It is what they understood.

When you disagree with a product decision, do you present a technical argument or do you present an alternative that addresses the same business goal? If the former, you are arguing on your terms instead of theirs.

Have you ever changed the direction of a meeting with a single statement? If not, you may be providing information without providing framing. Information is raw material. Framing is what makes it actionable.

Do you write design documents that non-engineers reference and share? If your documents only circulate within the engineering team, your written communication is not crossing the translation layer.

When someone asks you to explain a technical concept, do you reach for an analogy or do you reach for the precise definition? The precise definition serves engineers. The analogy serves everyone else. If you only have one mode, you are leaving half your audience behind.

After presenting a proposal that was declined, did you analyze whether the idea was wrong or whether the communication was wrong? These are different failure modes with different fixes. Most developers assume the idea lost on merit and never examine whether the packaging was the problem.

If more than half of these pointed toward communicating for engineers rather than for decisions, that is your gap. It is not a personality deficiency. It is an underdeveloped skill, no different from the first time you tried to write concurrent code or design a distributed system. You were not good at those things either, until you practiced.

The next chapter explores the challenge that makes communication even harder: the people on the other side of it, and what changes when your job shifts from managing systems to managing humans.

CHAPTER 4

Managing Humans

The Shift from Systems to People

The first time you manage another person, you realize something unsettling. People do not behave like systems.

Systems are predictable. You give them an input, you get an output. When something breaks, you trace the error, find the root cause, and fix it. The system does not have feelings about the fix. It does not push back. It does not lose motivation because you refactored its internals without asking first.

People are different in every way that matters.

They have context you cannot see. They have motivations that shift. They have bad days that have nothing to do with the codebase. They interpret the same words differently depending on when and how you say them. They remember how you made them feel long after they forget what you said.

Most developers who move into leadership roles are not prepared for this. They have spent years building a mental model for how systems work. They have gotten very good at reasoning about cause and effect in technical contexts. And then they are asked to apply that same rigor to human beings, and it falls apart immediately.

The mistake is not that they lack people skills. The mistake is that they try to manage people the way they manage systems. They look for root causes when someone is underperforming. They try to debug interpersonal conflicts with logic. They assume that if they explain something clearly enough, the other person will simply update their behavior like a service accepting a new configuration.

That is not how any of this works.

Managing people is a fundamentally different discipline. It requires empathy, patience, tolerance for ambiguity, and the willingness to sit with problems that do not have clean solutions. These are not skills most engineers practiced on the way up.

But they are the skills that separate good technical leaders from great ones.

Why Great Engineers Struggle with People

There is a specific reason why the best engineers often become the worst first-time managers. Their greatest strength becomes their biggest liability.

Engineers are trained to be right. The compiler does not care about your feelings. The test suite does not grade on effort. You either wrote correct code or you did not. Years of this training creates a mind that is optimized for precision, correctness, and efficiency. These are extraordinary qualities for building systems. They are terrible qualities for managing humans.

Here is where it breaks down.

Engineers optimize for speed. When they see someone struggling with a problem, their instinct is to jump in and solve it. This feels helpful. It is not. What it actually communicates is: I do not trust you to figure this out, so I am going to do it for you. The team member does not learn. They do not build confidence. And they start depending on you for every hard problem, which is the opposite of what a manager should create.

Engineers optimize for correctness. When someone brings an idea that is flawed, the engineer-turned-manager identifies the flaw immediately and points it out. This is technically correct and interpersonally destructive. The person who brought the idea hears: your thinking is wrong. Next time, they will not bring ideas. The manager has just killed the team's creative surface area in exchange for being right about one thing.

Engineers optimize for clarity. When expectations are not being met, they state the gap directly. "You said you would deliver by Friday. It is Monday and it is not done." This is factual. It is also useless as management. It tells the person what they already know without exploring why it happened, what got in the way, or what needs to change systemically. It is like printing an error log and handing it to the user. Technically accurate. Zero actionable information.

Engineers optimize for consistency. They create processes, templates, and standards. They want the team to operate like a well-designed system with predictable inputs and outputs. But teams are not systems. A process that works for a motivated senior engineer will suffocate a junior engineer who needs more context. A standard that serves the backend team may be completely wrong for the team working on experimental features. The manager who treats everyone the same way is not being fair. They are being lazy.

The transition from engineer to manager requires unlearning the instinct that made you successful. Not because those instincts are wrong. Because they were designed for a different problem space. Managing systems requires precision. Managing people requires judgment. And judgment means knowing when to be precise, when to be patient, and when to let someone find their own answer even though you already know it.

The Human Debugging Model

Engineers are not wrong to think of people problems analytically. The mistake is using the wrong debugging framework. Machines give you stack traces. People give you signals. The skill is learning to read those signals the way you learned to read logs.

Think of it as four steps. Signal, Behavior, Root Cause, Response.

Step one is Signal. Something catches your attention. A team member who used to contribute actively in design reviews has gone quiet. Someone who always shipped on time has missed two deadlines. A developer who used to write thoughtful code reviews is now approving everything with a thumbs up and no comments. These are signals. They are the human equivalent of a metric anomaly on your dashboard. They do not tell you what is wrong. They tell you something has changed.

Most managers miss signals because they are not looking for them. They are buried in their own work, looking at dashboards and roadmaps instead of looking at people. The first management skill worth developing is attention. Not surveillance. Attention. Knowing how your team normally operates well enough that you notice when something shifts.

Step two is Behavior. Once you notice a signal, observe the specific behavior without jumping to conclusions. The engineer who went quiet in design reviews is still writing code, still shipping, still present. But they have stopped engaging in collaborative discussions. That is the behavior. Not "they have checked out." Not "they do not care anymore." Just the observable behavior, stripped of your interpretation.

This distinction matters because your first interpretation is almost always wrong. The engineer who seems disengaged might be dealing with something personal. They might be frustrated with a recent decision that felt dismissive. They might be overwhelmed and triaging their energy. If you act on your interpretation instead of the observed behavior, you will address the wrong problem.

Step three is Root Cause. This is where you have a conversation. Not a confrontation. Not an interrogation. A genuine, curious conversation. The goal is not to prove your hypothesis. It is to understand theirs. "I have noticed you have been quieter in design reviews lately. I value your perspective in those discussions and wanted to check in. Is everything okay?"

That question does three things. It names the specific behavior without judgment. It communicates that you value their contribution. And it opens a door without forcing them through it. Sometimes the answer is simple: they have been heads down on a deadline and will re-engage next week. Sometimes the answer is complex: they feel like their input has been ignored in the last three reviews and they stopped seeing the point. Both answers are valuable. Neither would have surfaced without asking.

Root cause in people debugging is rarely a single variable. It is usually a combination of factors, some within your control and some not. Your job is not to find the one thing and fix it. Your job is to understand the landscape well enough to know where you can help.

Step four is Response. This is where most engineer-managers default to solutioning. They hear the problem and immediately propose a fix. Resist that instinct. The right response depends on what you learned in step three, and it is often not a solution at all. Sometimes the right response is acknowledgment. Sometimes it is removing an obstacle. Sometimes it is adjusting the work. Sometimes it is doing nothing except letting the person know you see them and you are available.

The Human Debugging Model does not always produce a fix. That is the point. People are not bugs. They are complex systems with state that you can only partially observe. The model gives you a structured way to engage without defaulting to the engineering instinct of diagnose-and-patch, which almost always makes things worse when applied to humans.

A High Performer Comes Apart

Raj was the strongest engineer on a platform team at a mid-size fintech company. For two years, he had been the person everyone turned to. He designed the event pipeline that handled millions of transactions daily. He mentored three junior developers. He wrote the technical RFCs that the architecture review board used as templates. His performance reviews were stellar. His manager, Chen, considered him the anchor of the team.

Then things started to shift.

It was gradual at first. Raj started declining invitations to architecture discussions. He said he was too deep in a migration project. Chen thought nothing of it. Raj's code output was still high. His PRs were still clean. Then Raj stopped mentoring. He told the juniors to pair with each other. Chen noticed but figured Raj was managing his energy during a busy stretch.

Six weeks later, Raj's code reviews became perfunctory. One-word approvals. No design feedback. His commit messages, which used to be detailed, became terse. He stopped attending optional meetings. He was still delivering, but the engagement was gone. The signal was everywhere, but Chen kept interpreting it as Raj being focused on the migration.

Chen finally brought it up in a one-on-one. He asked how the migration was going. Raj said fine. Chen asked about mentoring. Raj said the juniors were doing great on their own. Chen asked if everything was okay. Raj said yes.

That was the wrong question. It was closed, vague, and easy to deflect. Chen moved on to sprint planning.

Three months later, Raj gave his two-week notice. He was leaving for a smaller company. Chen was blindsided. In the exit interview, the HR lead shared the themes. Raj felt invisible. He had been carrying the hardest technical work for two years and watched two other people get promoted to staff engineer while he was told to "keep doing what you are doing." He had raised concerns about the event pipeline's scaling limitations six months ago in a design review. Nobody acted on them. He stopped bringing concerns because they did not seem to matter. He stopped mentoring because he felt like his growth was being sacrificed to support everyone else's.

Every signal was there. Raj's withdrawal was a textbook progression: reduced engagement in collaborative work, followed by reduced quality in peer contributions, followed by disengagement from the team's social fabric. Chen saw all of it and explained it away.

Where did the Human Debugging Model fail? It did not fail. It was never applied. Chen never moved past step one. He noticed the signals but interpreted them through the lens of "Raj is just busy." He never observed the behavior pattern with curiosity. He never had the real conversation. And his one-on-one question, "is everything okay," was step three done badly. It was a closed question with an obvious expected answer.

If Chen had applied the model, the intervention point was clear. After the second signal, declining mentoring, he should have named the pattern. "You have pulled back from reviews and mentoring in the last few weeks. That is different from your usual. I want to understand what is going on, because your perspective is something this team depends on." That opens the conversation. It names the behavior without judgment. It communicates value. And it gives Raj the space to say what he actually needs.

The hardest part of losing a high performer is that the warning signs were always visible. The cost is never just the departure. It is the six months of declining contribution before it, the institutional knowledge that walks out the door, and the team's morale hit when they see that the best among them was not taken care of.

A Conflict Becomes a Catalyst

Two engineers on a data platform team, Sana and Viktor, had a working relationship that was becoming toxic. Sana was a systems thinker. She wanted clean abstractions, well-defined interfaces, and documentation before implementation. Viktor was a pragmatist. He wanted to ship fast, iterate on feedback, and refactor later when the shape of the problem was clearer.

Their disagreements started in code reviews and escalated into design discussions. Sana would block Viktor's PRs for insufficient documentation. Viktor would push back publicly, calling the documentation requirements overhead that slowed the team. Other team members started avoiding topics that might trigger the conflict. The team's throughput dropped. Two junior developers asked to be reassigned.

Their manager, Leah, initially tried to stay out of it. She figured two senior engineers could work it out. When it became clear they could not, she tried the wrong intervention. She created a shared document of "team coding standards" and asked everyone to follow it. This made things worse. Sana treated the document as validation that her approach was correct. Viktor treated it as bureaucracy imposed without his input. The conflict deepened.

Leah realized her process-based fix had failed and decided to apply the debugging model.

Signal: obvious. The conflict was visible to the entire team. Behavior: Sana blocked PRs; Viktor pushed back publicly; the team had fractured into camps. Root cause: this was not about coding standards. Leah needed to go deeper.

She had separate one-on-ones with each of them. Not about the conflict directly. About their experience on the team.

Sana said she felt like the team was accumulating technical debt that nobody cared about. She had raised concerns in two retrospectives and nothing changed. Blocking PRs was the only lever she had to enforce quality. She knew it was creating friction, but she did not see another option.

Viktor said he felt like every initiative he drove was met with resistance. He had shipped three features in the last quarter, and each one had been delayed by review cycles that felt disproportionate. He cared about quality too, but he believed quality emerged from iteration, not from documentation that nobody read after it was written.

Leah saw the root cause clearly. Both engineers valued quality but defined it differently. Both felt powerless. Both had resorted to the tools available to them, PR blocking and public pushback, because they did not have a structured way to resolve their fundamental disagreement about how the team should work.

The response was not a process. It was a conversation. Leah brought Sana and Viktor together and framed it differently than they expected. She did not ask them to compromise. She asked them to design a system together. "You both care about quality and speed. Those are not actually in conflict. The question is: where in our workflow should quality checks happen, and what form should they take? I want you two to own the answer."

She gave them a week. They came back with a proposal that neither of them would have created alone. Lightweight design docs for anything touching shared interfaces. Fast-path approvals for isolated changes. A weekly "architecture health" discussion where concerns like Sana's could be raised before they became PR-level battles. Viktor liked it because it removed blocking from the critical path. Sana liked it because it gave her a real forum for the concerns she had been raising through code reviews.

Within a month, the team's throughput recovered. Within two months, it exceeded the pre-conflict baseline. The junior developers came back. And Sana and Viktor, who had been adversaries, became the team's most effective design partnership.

Leah did not fix the conflict by picking a side or imposing a standard. She used the debugging model to understand what was underneath the visible behavior, and then she responded with a structural change that addressed the root cause. She turned a management problem into a team-level improvement. That is what people management looks like when it is done well. Not policing behavior. Not avoiding conflict. Channeling the energy behind the conflict toward something productive.

What Most Developers Get Wrong About Management

Three misconceptions keep engineers from becoming effective managers.

The first is thinking management is about control. Engineers come from a world where they have direct control over the system. You write the code. You choose the architecture. You decide the implementation. Management looks like a higher level of control. You set the direction. You assign the work. You evaluate the output. But the best managers do not control their teams. They create conditions. They create the environment, the clarity, and the support system that allows talented people to do their best work. The more you try to control, the more you constrain. The more you enable, the more you multiply.

The second is thinking feedback is optional. Many engineer-managers treat feedback as something that happens in performance reviews, twice a year, when HR requires it. This is catastrophic. By the time you deliver feedback in a formal review, the behavior has been reinforced for months. The person either does not remember the specific instance or has come to believe the behavior is acceptable because nobody said anything. Feedback is not an event. It is a practice. It happens in the moment, in one-on-ones, in code reviews, in design discussions. The managers who give feedback consistently create teams that improve continuously. The managers who save it create teams that are surprised twice a year.

The third is thinking the best managers were born with people skills. This is the most damaging misconception because it lets engineers off the hook. If management is a talent, then either you have it or you do not, and there is nothing to practice. But management is not a talent. It is a skill set. Active listening is a skill. Giving feedback is a skill. Running a productive one-on-one is a skill. Navigating conflict is a skill. Every one of these can be studied, practiced, and improved. The engineer who approaches management with the same deliberate practice they applied to learning a programming language will get better at it. The engineer who assumes it is innate will not.

Psychological Safety Is Not a Buzzword

There is a term that gets thrown around so often that it has almost lost its meaning. Psychological safety. It sounds corporate. It sounds like something from a training slide deck. Most engineers hear it and file it under things that do not affect real work.

That is a mistake.

Psychological safety is the single most predictive factor in team performance. Google studied this extensively in their Project Aristotle research. The highest-performing teams were not the ones with the smartest individuals or the best technical skills. They were the teams where people felt safe to speak up, admit mistakes, and challenge each other without fear of punishment.

Think about what that means in an engineering context. A team without psychological safety is a team where bugs get hidden instead of reported. Where junior developers copy and paste from Stack Overflow instead of asking questions. Where architects make decisions in isolation because challenging them feels risky. Where the person who sees the design flaw stays quiet because the last time someone raised a concern, the lead dismissed them in front of the group.

These are not abstract scenarios. They happen in engineering teams every day. And they are invisible to the manager who is not paying attention.

Building psychological safety does not mean being nice. It does not mean avoiding conflict. It means creating an environment where honesty is rewarded rather than punished. Where admitting you do not know something is treated as a sign of maturity, not weakness. Where disagreement is seen as a signal of engagement, not disloyalty.

This starts with you. If you react defensively when someone challenges your idea, the team learns not to challenge ideas. If you punish failure, the team learns not to take risks. If you dismiss concerns, the team learns not to raise them.

You set the tone. Every reaction teaches the team what is safe and what is not. And once trust is broken, it takes a very long time to rebuild.

Giving Feedback That Actually Changes Behavior

Most developers give terrible feedback. Not because they are unkind, but because they approach feedback the way they approach code reviews. Here is what is wrong. Here is how to fix it. Move on.

That works for code. It does not work for people.

Effective feedback has three components. It is specific, it is timely, and it connects to something the person cares about.

Specific means you reference a concrete behavior, not a general trait. "Your code reviews are too slow" is not feedback. "The last three pull requests you reviewed sat for four days before you responded, which blocked the team from shipping" is feedback. The first sounds like a judgment. The second sounds like an observation. People can work with observations. Judgments make them defensive.

Timely means you deliver the feedback close to the event. Not in a quarterly review three months later. Not in a one-on-one two weeks after the incident. As close to the moment as possible, while the context is still fresh. The longer you wait, the more abstract the feedback becomes, and the harder it is for the person to connect it to their actual behavior.

Connected means the feedback ties to something the person values. If someone cares about being a strong technical contributor, frame the feedback in terms of how their behavior affects technical outcomes. If someone cares about the team, frame it in terms of team impact. You are not manipulating. You are translating. The same behavior can be described through different lenses. Choose the lens that resonates.

There is one more thing that most new managers get wrong. They only give feedback when something is wrong.

Positive feedback is not a participation trophy. It is a calibration tool. When you tell someone specifically what they did well and why it mattered, you are showing them what good looks like. You are reinforcing the behaviors you want to see more of. You are giving them data about what success means on this team.

The managers who only surface problems create teams that are anxious and uncertain. The managers who balance correction with recognition create teams that improve fast because people understand the target they are aiming for.

Running One-on-Ones That Matter

Most one-on-ones are wasted time. The manager asks "how are things going?" The engineer says "fine." They review the sprint board for fifteen minutes. Nothing meaningful happens. Both leave feeling like the meeting could have been a Slack message.

This is a failure of structure, not intent.

A good one-on-one is not a status update. Status should live in tickets, standups, and dashboards. The one-on-one exists for something different. It is the space where you learn things that do not show up in the project tracker. Where you hear that someone is frustrated with a process. Where you catch early signs that someone is burning out. Where you give the kind of nuanced feedback that does not belong in a public channel.

The most effective format is simple. Let the person set the agenda. They bring the topics that matter to them. You listen more than you talk. You ask questions that go deeper than the surface. "How is the project going?" is a weak question. "What is the hardest part of the project right now, and what would make it easier?" is a question that actually gets you somewhere.

Some one-on-ones will be short. That is fine. If the person is doing well and has nothing to discuss, a ten-minute check-in is perfectly adequate. But the space needs to exist. Because the week they do have something to talk about, something hard, something personal, something that is affecting their work, the trust and the habit need to already be there.

The biggest mistake managers make with one-on-ones is treating them as optional. They cancel when the calendar gets busy. They reschedule repeatedly. They show up distracted.

Every time you cancel a one-on-one, you are sending a message. You are telling that person that their time and their concerns are less important than whatever else is on your calendar. Do that enough times and they stop bringing up the things that matter. They stop trusting that you are invested in their growth.

And then you wonder why they leave.

What to Do Monday Morning

Start with your one-on-ones. If you do not have them, schedule them. If you have them but they have become status updates, restructure them this week.

Here is a format that works. Open with one question: "What is the most important thing we should talk about today?" Then be quiet. Let the person fill the space. If they say "nothing," do not accept it. Follow up with: "What has been the hardest part of your week?" or "Is there anything that has been frustrating you that I might not be aware of?" These are not therapy questions. They are management questions. They surface the problems that project trackers cannot capture.

In the middle of the conversation, look for one opportunity to give specific feedback. Not generic praise. Not vague criticism. Something concrete. Here is an example of what that sounds like.

"In the design review on Tuesday, you raised the concern about the API rate limits before anyone else had thought about it. That saved the team from a problem that would have shown up in production. That is exactly the kind of upstream thinking I want to see more of from you."

That is specific. It references a concrete event. It names the behavior. It explains the impact. And it tells the person what good looks like. It took ten seconds to say. It will shape their behavior for weeks.

Close with alignment. "Is there anything you need from me this week?" This is not a formality. This is the manager's job distilled to one question. Your role is to remove obstacles and provide what your team needs to do their best work. Asking it explicitly and following through on the answer builds the trust that makes everything else work.

If someone on your team is struggling, apply the Human Debugging Model this week. Start with step one. What signals are you noticing? Write them down. Then observe the behavior without interpreting it. Then have the conversation. Not "is everything okay?" but "I have noticed [specific behavior] and I want to understand what is going on."

Do not try to fix anything in the first conversation. Just listen. The act of genuinely listening, without jumping to solutions, is so rare in engineering management that it is often the intervention itself.

Motivating Different Types of Engineers

Not every engineer is motivated by the same thing. This sounds obvious, but most managers act as if it is not true. They apply the same approach to everyone. More ownership. More challenging technical work. More visibility.

For some engineers, that is exactly right. For others, it is exactly wrong.

Some developers are motivated by craft. They want to write elegant, well-tested code. They care about design patterns and system purity. Giving them a messy, deadline-driven project with no time for quality will drain them.

Some developers are motivated by impact. They want to ship things that users interact with. They care about the outcome, not the implementation. Putting them on an internal infrastructure project with no visible user impact will bore them.

Some developers are motivated by learning. They want to work on things they have never done before. Repetitive work, even if it is important, will make them restless.

Some developers are motivated by stability. They want clear expectations, consistent processes, and predictable work. Constant change and ambiguity will stress them out.

The mistake is assuming your own motivation applies to everyone. Most new managers default to managing the way they would want to be managed. But you are not managing yourself. You are managing individuals with different histories, different goals, and different definitions of fulfillment.

The only way to learn what motivates someone is to ask. And then to listen. Not to the surface answer, but to the pattern underneath. Watch what energizes them. Watch what drains them. Pay attention to the projects they volunteer for and the ones they avoid.

Once you understand what drives each person, you can create alignment. Match the right person to the right work. Frame challenges in terms that resonate with their values. Remove the things that sap their energy.

This is not about being a therapist. It is about being a thoughtful allocator of human capacity. You are running a system, but the components have preferences, emotions, and aspirations. The manager who ignores that will get compliance. The manager who works with it will get commitment.

That is the difference.

Checklist: Are You Managing Tasks or People?

Before moving to the next chapter, run through this honestly.

When a team member misses a deadline, do you focus on the missed date or on understanding why it happened? If you focus on the date, you are managing output, not people. Deadlines are symptoms. Causes live underneath.

In your last one-on-one, did you spend more time reviewing the sprint board or listening to what the person wanted to talk about? If the sprint board won, your one-on-ones are status meetings, not management conversations.

Can you name the primary motivation of each person on your team, whether it is craft, impact, learning, or stability? If you cannot, you are managing everyone the same way, which means you are managing no one well.

When was the last time you gave positive feedback that was specific enough that the person knew exactly what behavior to repeat? If you cannot remember, your team does not have a clear picture of what success looks like.

Have you noticed any signals from your team in the last two weeks, a change in engagement, a shift in energy, a withdrawal from collaboration? If you have not noticed anything, you are either not looking or not present enough to see.

When two people on your team disagree, do you resolve it by picking a side, imposing a process, or helping them understand each other's perspective? If you default to process, you are managing the symptom, not the relationship.

Do your team members bring you problems early, or do you find out about issues late? If problems arrive late, your team does not feel safe enough to surface them. That is a psychological safety gap, and it is on you.

Could someone on your team describe your management approach in terms that go beyond "they are nice" or "they leave me alone"? If not, you have not made your values and expectations explicit enough for people to work with.

If more than half of these pointed toward managing tasks, that is a signal worth paying attention to. You are not failing. You are defaulting to what engineering trained you to do. The shift from managing tasks to managing people is not intuitive. It is learned. And it starts with one honest one-on-one, one real conversation, one moment where you choose to listen instead of solve.

The next chapter explores the skill that makes all of this scale: thinking in systems, not just building them.

CHAPTER 5

Thinking in Systems

The Feature Factory

Most engineering teams operate the same way. Product defines a roadmap. Engineering breaks it into features. Features become tickets. Tickets become sprints. Sprints become releases. Releases become metrics that justify the next round of features.

This cycle feels productive. Things are shipping. Dashboards are updating. Stakeholders are getting demos. Everyone is busy.

But something is off.

The product keeps growing, but it does not feel like it is getting better. New features introduce unexpected bugs in unrelated areas. Performance degrades with every release. The codebase becomes harder to change. Developers spend more time working around existing code than writing new code. Every project takes longer than the last one, and nobody can explain exactly why.

This is what happens when teams think in features instead of systems.

Feature thinking is linear. You have a request. You build it. You ship it. You move to the next one. Each feature is treated as an independent unit of work with its own requirements, its own timeline, and its own definition of done.

System thinking is different. It recognizes that every feature exists inside a larger whole. It asks how a new addition interacts with everything that already exists. It considers not just what will happen when the feature works correctly, but what will happen when it fails, when it scales, when it is maintained by someone who did not build it, and when the assumptions behind it change.

Most developers are naturally good at system thinking within code. They understand dependency management, interface contracts, and separation of concerns. But they rarely apply that same thinking to the product, the organization, or the business.

That is where the real leverage is.

Why Feature Thinking Breaks at Scale

Feature thinking works when the system is small. When you have one team, one codebase, and a product that fits in your head, you can reason about features independently because you already understand the whole. You can hold the entire system in working memory while you design and build the next piece.

That stops working somewhere around the third team, the second year, or the hundredth feature. Pick your threshold. The point is that every system crosses a line where feature-level reasoning produces system-level failures. And nobody sends you a notification when you cross it.

Here is why. Features interact. Not just technically, but behaviorally. A search feature and a recommendation feature are independent in the codebase. But they compete for the same user attention on the same page. The search team optimizes for relevance. The recommendation team optimizes for discovery. Neither team is wrong. But the user sees a page that is pulling them in two directions, and the experience degrades in a way that no single team's metrics capture.

Features share resources. Your shiny new real-time analytics dashboard and the batch processing job that generates monthly reports both hit the same database. Both passed load testing individually. Neither was tested alongside the other. On the first of the month, when the batch job runs during peak dashboard hours, the database buckles. The incident is not a bug in either feature. It is a system-level failure that only exists because both features exist.

Features create expectations. Every feature you ship teaches users and stakeholders to expect more. The feature that lets users export data to CSV creates the expectation that they can export to Excel. The feature that sends email notifications creates the expectation that they can choose Slack instead. Each feature is not just a piece of functionality. It is a promise of further investment, and the cumulative weight of those promises consumes more engineering capacity than the features themselves.

Features compound complexity. This is the most insidious problem. Each feature, individually, is manageable. But features do not add complexity linearly. They multiply it. Every new feature interacts with every existing feature. A system with ten features does not have ten units of complexity. It has something closer to a hundred, because every feature has potential interactions with every other feature. A system with a hundred features has potential interactions in the thousands. This is why mature products feel heavy. The features are fine. The interactions are crushing.

The developer who thinks in features will keep building clean, well-tested features that make the system worse. The developer who thinks in systems will pause and ask: what happens when this feature meets everything else we have already built?

The System Lens

When system thinking feels abstract, it helps to have a concrete tool. The System Lens gives you four questions to ask before building anything that touches more than your own component. These are not theoretical. They are practical checkpoints that surface the risks feature thinking misses.

The first lens is Inputs. Where does the data come from? Who produces it? What assumptions are we making about its format, frequency, and reliability? Most features treat their inputs as a given. The system thinker traces inputs back to their source and asks what happens when that source changes. A team building a personalization engine that relies on user clickstream data needs to know that the analytics team is planning to migrate their event pipeline next quarter. A feature that depends on a third-party API needs to account for the rate limits, latency characteristics, and deprecation timeline of that API. Inputs that seem stable are often the first things that change, and features built on unstable inputs fail in ways that look random and are painful to debug.

The second lens is Dependencies. What does this feature depend on that your team does not control? This goes beyond technical dependencies. Organizational dependencies are the ones that cause the most damage. If your feature requires the mobile team to update their SDK, and the mobile team is mid-release with a freeze on non-critical changes, your feature is blocked by a dependency that does not show up in any architecture diagram. Process dependencies matter too. If launching your feature requires a security review, and the security team has a three-week backlog, that review is a dependency on your timeline regardless of how fast your engineering work is. The developer who maps dependencies before writing code avoids the surprise blockers that derail projects in the final stretch.

The third lens is Trade-offs. What are you optimizing for, and what are you sacrificing? Every feature involves trade-offs. Speed versus thoroughness. Flexibility versus simplicity. User experience versus system performance. The system thinker makes these trade-offs explicit before building, not after shipping. They name the trade-off out loud in the planning meeting. They write it in the design document. They make sure the team and the stakeholders understand what is being gained and what is being given up. A trade-off that is named can be managed. A trade-off that is implicit becomes a surprise when the sacrificed value shows up as a problem.

The fourth lens is Outcomes. What does this feature produce, and who consumes those outputs? This is not the same as asking what the feature does. It is asking how the feature's existence changes the behavior of the rest of the system. A feature that generates notifications produces load on the notification infrastructure. A feature that creates new data produces storage costs and new query patterns. A feature that changes a user workflow produces retraining needs and support ticket volume. The outputs of your feature become the inputs of other systems, other teams, and other people's plans. The developer who traces outputs downstream catches the problems that surface weeks after launch, the ones that are technically somebody else's problem but are really yours because your feature created them.

The four lenses are not a gate to pass. They are a way of seeing. Once you start asking these questions habitually, you stop treating features as independent units and start seeing them as nodes in a living system. That perspective is what separates engineers who build features from engineers who build products.

The Feature That Broke the System

A growth team at a SaaS company was tasked with improving trial-to-paid conversion. They analyzed the data and identified that users who invited team members during their trial were three times more likely to convert.

The insight was solid. The solution seemed obvious. Make team invitations easier and more prominent.

The team built a beautiful invitation flow. They added prompts during onboarding. They created an in-app nudge that appeared after the user completed their first project. They sent automated emails at day three and day seven suggesting the user invite colleagues. They A/B tested the messaging. They optimized the placement. By every growth metric, the feature was a success. Invitations during trial increased by 140 percent in the first month.

Then the downstream effects started appearing.

The first problem was infrastructure. The invitation emails and in-app notifications created a significant spike in the messaging queue. The messaging service, which was shared across the entire platform, started showing increased latency. Transactional emails like password resets and billing confirmations were delayed by minutes during peak hours. The infrastructure team traced the issue to the invitation volume and filed a bug against the growth team. The growth team said the messaging service should be able to handle the load. The infrastructure team said the growth team should have coordinated before tripling their message volume overnight. Both were right. Neither had talked to the other before launch.

The second problem was billing. When trial users invited team members, those members got full access to the trial workspace. When the trial converted to a paid plan, the billing system calculated the seat count based on active users. Trial users who had invited eight colleagues were shocked by their first invoice. Support tickets about unexpected charges increased by 60 percent. The billing team had not been consulted about the invitation flow because the growth team did not think of billing as a dependency. It was not a technical dependency. It was a business logic dependency that nobody mapped.

The third problem was retention. The growth team's hypothesis was correct. Users who invited team members were more likely to convert. But the data hid an important nuance. Users who organically invited team members were more likely to convert because the invitation was a signal of genuine engagement. Users who were prompted to invite team members were often complying with a nudge rather than expressing real intent. Their invitees were less engaged. Their workspaces were less active. Their 90-day retention was significantly lower than the organic inviter cohort. The feature had successfully moved a metric while undermining the business outcome the metric was supposed to represent.

None of these problems were bugs. The invitation feature worked exactly as designed. The failures were systemic. They happened at the boundaries between the feature and the rest of the platform. They happened because the team applied all four lenses of feature thinking, requirements, design, implementation, testing, and none of the four lenses of system thinking.

If the team had used the System Lens, the intervention points were clear. Inputs: what messaging infrastructure are we relying on, and can it handle the projected volume? Dependencies: who else is affected by changes to the invitation flow, particularly billing and the infrastructure team? Trade-offs: are we optimizing for invitation volume at the expense of invitation quality? Outcomes: what downstream effects does a tripled invitation volume create for other teams and systems?

Any one of those questions, asked before launch, would have changed the plan. Not killed it. Improved it. The system thinker does not stop features from shipping. They stop features from shipping damage.

What Most Developers Miss About Systems

Three blind spots prevent most developers from thinking systemically, even developers who are strong system designers within their own codebase.

The first blind spot is boundaries. Developers naturally think about the systems they own. Their service. Their API. Their database. System thinking starts at the edges of what you own and extends outward. The most important system behaviors happen at the boundaries between teams, between services, between your code and someone else's process. A service that performs beautifully in isolation but creates a bottleneck for three downstream consumers is not a well-designed system. It is a well-designed component inside a poorly understood system. Seeing past the boundaries of your ownership is the first step to thinking in systems.

The second blind spot is time. Developers evaluate systems at a point in time. They ask: does this work now? System thinking requires asking: what happens to this over time? Code that works today but requires manual intervention as data grows is a system that degrades. An architecture that performs well at current scale but has a hard ceiling at ten times the load is a system with a time bomb. A dependency on a vendor that is financially unstable is a system with a risk that no load test will reveal. Most system failures are not sudden. They are gradual. They emerge over weeks and months as conditions change and assumptions erode. The developer who factors time into their system analysis catches these slow failures before they become crises.

The third blind spot is incentives. Every system includes the people who operate it, and people respond to incentives. If the on-call rotation penalizes the team that owns the most complex service, engineers will avoid owning complex services, and critical infrastructure will be understaffed. If the promotion criteria reward feature velocity, engineers will optimize for shipping over stability, and system quality will decline. If the code review process is cumbersome, engineers will make fewer, larger PRs, and integration risk will increase. These are system dynamics that have nothing to do with code. But they shape code outcomes more than any architectural decision. The developer who can see incentive structures as part of the system, not separate from it, understands why good engineers sometimes produce bad systems. The code is a symptom. The incentives are the cause.

Second-Order Effects

Every decision has consequences. First-order effects are the ones you intended. Second-order effects are the ones you did not plan for.

Most teams are good at reasoning about first-order effects. We add caching, so reads get faster. We introduce a new microservice, so this component can scale independently. We automate this process, so the team saves two hours a week.

Second-order effects are harder. They emerge over time, and they often contradict the original intent.

We add caching, so reads get faster. But now we have a cache invalidation problem that introduces subtle data consistency bugs. Developers start spending time debugging stale data issues. The team adds more cache logic to handle edge cases. The caching layer becomes the most complex part of the system. A year later, someone proposes removing the cache entirely because it causes more problems than it solves.

This is not a failure of the original decision. It is a failure to think beyond the first order. And it is one of the most common patterns in software engineering. Teams solve a problem, create a new one, solve that one, create another, and eventually the system is more patch than product.

Second-order thinking does not mean you predict the future perfectly. It means you ask: and then what? You follow the chain of consequences one or two steps further than most people do. You consider not just the direct impact of a decision but the behavioral changes it will trigger.

When you add a feature flag system, the first-order effect is more deployment flexibility. The second-order effect is that flag cleanup becomes a maintenance burden, and if nobody owns it, the system accumulates hundreds of stale flags that make the code harder to reason about.

When you split a monolith into microservices, the first-order effect is independent deployability. The second-order effect is distributed system complexity, network reliability concerns, and a coordination overhead that can slow down feature development more than the monolith ever did.

The developer who thinks in second-order effects does not reject these decisions. They anticipate the downstream consequences and plan for them. They propose the migration and the cleanup strategy in the same conversation. They advocate for the architecture change and the operational investment it will require.

This is system thinking applied to decision-making. It is the difference between solving today's problem and solving today's problem without creating three new ones for next quarter.

Trade-offs at Scale

Early in your career, trade-offs feel small. Do you use a list or a hash map? Do you optimize for read speed or write speed? Do you add the feature now or refactor first?

At scale, trade-offs become much larger and much less reversible.

Do you build your own infrastructure or buy from a vendor? Do you invest in platform reliability or new feature development? Do you standardize on one technology stack or let teams choose their own? Do you hire more engineers or invest in tooling that makes the current team more productive?

These decisions do not have correct answers. They have different sets of consequences, and the right choice depends on context that changes over time. What was right for a twenty-person startup is wrong for a five-hundred-person company. What was right last year might be wrong this year because the market shifted.

Most developers are not trained to think about trade-offs at this level. They are trained to find the best solution. The optimal algorithm. The cleanest architecture. The right answer.

But at scale, there is no right answer. There are only trade-offs that you understand and trade-offs that you do not.

The strategic developer makes trade-offs explicit. They name what is being gained and what is being given up. They make sure the team and the stakeholders understand the constraints. They do not pretend that a decision is purely technical when it has business implications, and they do not pretend a business decision has no technical cost.

This is harder than it sounds because it requires you to give up the comfort of certainty. Engineers love certainty. They love provable correctness and deterministic outcomes. Trade-off analysis at scale offers neither. It offers judgment, probability, and the willingness to be wrong and adapt.

The practical discipline here is to always state what you are optimizing for and what you are sacrificing. "We are optimizing for time-to-market, which means we are accepting higher maintenance cost in six months." "We are optimizing for data consistency, which means we are accepting higher latency on writes." These statements feel obvious once they are said out loud. But most teams never say them out loud. They make the choice implicitly and then act surprised when the sacrificed value shows up as a problem later.

Naming the trade-off does not make the decision easier. But it makes the decision honest. And honest decisions are the ones that organizations can learn from.

Avoiding Local Optimization

There is a pattern in engineering teams that is so common it has become invisible. Each team optimizes for their own metrics, their own velocity, their own goals. And the system as a whole gets worse.

The platform team optimizes for stability and ships fewer changes. The product team optimizes for feature velocity and demands faster releases.

The security team optimizes for risk reduction and adds friction to every deployment. Each team is doing the right thing by their own measure. But the combination creates an organization that moves slowly, fights constantly, and produces mediocre outcomes.

This is local optimization. Each component performs well in isolation. The system performs poorly as a whole.

Developers who think in features fall into this trap naturally. They optimize the code they own. They make their service faster, their API cleaner, their deployment pipeline smoother. But they do not ask whether their optimization is creating a bottleneck for someone else.

Developers who think in systems ask a different question. They ask: what is the constraint of the overall system, and how does my work affect it?

Sometimes the answer is that the constraint is not in your code at all. The system is slow because of a handoff between teams. The product is unreliable because of a shared dependency that nobody owns. The organization ships slowly because the approval process has more steps than the deployment pipeline.

The developer who can see the whole system and identify the actual bottleneck is worth more than the developer who perfectly optimizes their own component. Because improving a non-bottleneck has zero impact on the system's overall performance. All the effort goes into making something faster that was never the thing slowing you down.

This is one of the most counterintuitive lessons in system thinking. Doing excellent work on the wrong thing produces zero value. The constraint is the constraint. Everything else is noise.

What to Do Monday Morning

Before you start building your next feature, draw the dependency map. Not the technical architecture diagram. The real dependency map.

Take fifteen minutes with a blank document. Write the name of the feature or project at the center. Then answer four questions, one for each lens.

Inputs: where does the data or trigger for this feature originate? Who owns that source? What are they planning to change in the next quarter? If you do not know, that is your first conversation.

Dependencies: what does this feature need from teams or systems outside your control? List every team that will need to review, approve, update, or accommodate your work. If the list is longer than two, your timeline is at risk, and you should communicate that now rather than discover it later.

Trade-offs: what are you optimizing for? Write it down as a sentence that starts with "We are optimizing for..." and ends with "which means we are accepting..." If you cannot finish that sentence, you have not made the trade-off explicit, which means the team will discover it later as a surprise.

Outcomes: what does this feature produce that other systems or teams will consume? Will it generate new data, new load, new user expectations, new support volume? Who downstream needs to know this feature is coming?

You do not need permission to do this exercise. You do not need a meeting. You need fifteen minutes and a willingness to think beyond the boundary of your own code. If the exercise surfaces a risk or a dependency you did not know about, share it with the team. That single act, surfacing a system-level concern that nobody else had mapped, is the highest-leverage contribution you can make in most planning cycles. It does not require seniority. It requires attention.

Over time, this habit reshapes how the team plans. Other engineers see you mapping dependencies and start doing it themselves. Product managers start asking about downstream effects because you taught them to expect the question. The planning process gets better because one person decided to look past the feature and see the system.

That is how system thinking spreads. Not through mandates. Through example.

Checklist: Are You Solving Locally or System-Wide?

Before moving to the next chapter, run through this honestly.

When you design a feature, do you trace your inputs back to their source and verify the assumptions you are making about them? If not, you are building on ground you have not inspected.

Can you list every team outside your own that will be affected by your current project? If the list is blank or has one entry, you are either working on something truly isolated or you have not looked far enough.

Before your last major technical decision, did you state explicitly what you were optimizing for and what you were sacrificing? If the trade-off was implicit, it will surface later as a surprise. Surprises in production are always more expensive than conversations in planning.

When you shipped your last feature, did you consider the second-order effects? Not just what the feature does, but what behaviors and dependencies it creates? If you stopped at first-order reasoning, you solved today's problem and may have seeded next quarter's.

Do you know the top constraint in your overall system, the thing that actually limits throughput for the organization? If you are optimizing something that is not the constraint, your excellent work is producing zero system-level value.

Have you looked at the dependency map for your current project, including organizational and process dependencies, not just technical ones? If your map only shows services and APIs, it is missing the dependencies that are most likely to block you.

When another team ships something that affects your system, are you surprised, or did you know it was coming? If you are regularly surprised by changes from other teams, you are operating in a silo, and your system model is incomplete.

In the last month, have you raised a system-level concern in a planning discussion, something that went beyond your own component? If not, you are thinking locally even when the risks are global.

If more than half of these pointed toward local thinking, that is not a failure. It is the default mode for most engineers. Feature thinking is what the process rewards, what the tickets encourage, and what the sprint structure reinforces. Thinking in systems requires deliberate effort against that current. But the engineers who make that effort are the ones who prevent the failures that nobody else sees coming, and that prevention, invisible as it is, is worth more than any feature shipped on time.

The next chapter examines the skill that ties system thinking to leadership: decision-making under uncertainty, and what changes when you have to choose without all the information.

CHAPTER 6

Decision Making Under Uncertainty

The Comfortable Illusion of Complete Information

Engineers are trained to gather requirements before they build. Define the inputs. Specify the outputs. Map the edge cases. Understand the constraints. Then execute.

This works beautifully inside a codebase. The compiler does not deal in ambiguity. The test suite does not accept "probably correct." The system either works or it does not.

But the decisions that matter most in your career will never have complete information. You will not know whether the market will shift. You will not know whether the team can deliver on the timeline. You will not know if the architecture will hold under load patterns that do not exist yet. You will not know if the competitor is six months ahead or six months behind.

And you will have to decide anyway.

This is where most developers freeze. They ask for more data. They run another analysis. They build a prototype to test a hypothesis. They schedule another meeting to gather input. All of these are reasonable actions. But at some point, every one of them becomes a form of avoidance.

The uncomfortable truth is that waiting for complete information is itself a decision. It is a decision to delay. And delay has a cost that most people never calculate. While you are gathering more data, the market moves. The team loses momentum. The window of opportunity narrows. The competitor ships.

The developers who become effective leaders learn to operate in the gap between what they know and what they need to know. They do not pretend uncertainty does not exist. They do not make reckless guesses. They develop a discipline for making sound decisions with imperfect information, and they get comfortable with the possibility of being wrong.

That comfort is not natural for engineers. It has to be built deliberately, the same way you built your debugging instinct or your sense for code quality. It is a skill, not a personality trait. And the developers who build it early gain an enormous advantage over those who keep waiting for the data to make the decision for them.

Why Engineers Struggle with Ambiguity

There is a reason this is so hard for technically trained people, and it goes deeper than personality.

Engineering education rewards precision. Every exam has a correct answer. Every proof has a definitive conclusion. Every algorithm has a measurable performance characteristic. You spend years learning that rigor is the path to correctness, and correctness is the goal. Then you enter an organization and discover that most of the important questions do not have correct answers.

Should we enter this market? Should we hire for this role or that one? Should we invest in reliability or features this quarter? Should we build this ourselves or partner with a vendor?

These are judgment calls. They depend on values, priorities, context, and prediction. Two smart people with the same information can reasonably reach different conclusions. That feels wrong to an engineer. It feels like someone must be making an error.

But nobody is making an error. They are weighing trade-offs differently because they have different mental models of what matters. And that is exactly what organizational decision-making looks like.

There are three specific ways the engineering mindset creates friction with ambiguity.

The first is the search for the optimal solution. Engineers are trained to find the best answer. The most efficient algorithm. The cleanest architecture. The correct approach. In ambiguous environments, there is no optimal solution. There are only acceptable options with different risk profiles. The engineer who keeps searching for the best answer when several good-enough answers exist is burning time that the organization cannot afford.

The second is the need for completeness. Engineers want to understand the full problem before proposing a solution. In code, that is wisdom. In organizations, it is paralysis. The full problem is never fully knowable. New information arrives constantly. Conditions change between the start and end of your analysis. The engineer who waits to understand everything before acting will always be acting on information that has already begun to decay.

The third is the aversion to being wrong. Engineers build their professional identity around correctness. Being the person who catches the bug. Being the person whose design holds up under load. Being the person whose technical judgment is reliable. That identity becomes a liability in ambiguous environments because it makes you reluctant to commit to a position that might turn out to be wrong. And in ambiguous environments, every position might turn out to be wrong. The question is not whether you will be wrong. It is how quickly you will recognize it and adjust.

The developer who learns to synthesize incomplete information, form a position, and advocate for it clearly is the one who moves things forward. This does not mean abandoning rigor. It means applying rigor to a different kind of problem. Instead of proving correctness, you are estimating likelihood. Instead of finding the optimal solution, you are finding the best available option given current constraints. Instead of eliminating uncertainty, you are managing it.

That is a fundamentally different intellectual discipline. And most engineers have never been taught how to practice it.

The 70% Decision Rule

Here is a practical threshold that changes how you make decisions. If you have 70 percent of the information you wish you had, decide.

Not 100 percent. Not 90 percent. Seventy.

This number is not arbitrary. Below 70 percent, you are genuinely guessing. You do not have enough signal to form a defensible position. The risk of a bad outcome is high, and the cost of gathering a bit more information is worth it.

Above 70 percent, you are in the zone of diminishing returns. Each additional piece of information takes longer to acquire and changes the decision less. The gap between 70 and 90 percent of information rarely changes the direction. It only increases your confidence in a direction you were already leaning toward. And confidence is not the same as correctness.

The cost of moving from 70 to 90 percent confidence is usually measured in weeks. Weeks of analysis, additional meetings, prototypes, and stakeholder alignment. During those weeks, the environment changes. Competitors move. Customer needs shift. Team momentum dissipates. The window for the decision may narrow or close entirely.

The 70% Rule does not mean being reckless. It means being honest about the gap between the information you have and the information you want, and recognizing that the gap will never fully close. The question is not "do I know enough?" It is "do I know enough to make a decision that is better than not deciding?"

Here is what the 70% Rule looks like in practice. Your team is evaluating two approaches to a data migration. Approach A is faster but riskier. Approach B is safer but takes three weeks longer. You have benchmarks for both, but the benchmarks are based on test data that does not fully represent production patterns. You could spend two weeks building a more realistic test harness. Or you can look at the benchmarks you have, assess the risk tolerance of the project, and choose.

If the migration is reversible and the risk of approach A is limited to a recoverable failure, the 70% Rule says decide now. Choose A, ship it, monitor closely, and be ready to switch to B if the risk materializes. You will have real production data in days, which is worth more than any test harness you could build.

If the migration is irreversible and a failure means data loss, the calculus is different. That is not a 70 percent decision. That is a decision that warrants the extra two weeks.

The 70% Rule is not a universal prescription. It is a bias toward action that counterbalances the engineer's natural bias toward analysis. Most engineers err on the side of gathering more information. The 70% Rule gives you permission to err on the side of deciding, with the understanding that you will learn more from the outcome than from any further analysis.

The best decision-makers are not the ones who are right most often. They are the ones who decide at 70 percent, learn from the result, and adjust faster than everyone else.

Reversible vs Irreversible Decisions

The 70% Rule works because most decisions are not permanent. But to apply it well, you need to know which decisions can be undone and which cannot. This distinction is the most powerful simplification in decision-making.

A reversible decision is one where the cost of being wrong is low and the ability to change course is high. Choosing a UI framework for an internal tool. Trying a new sprint format. Launching a feature behind a feature flag. Restructuring a team's standup cadence. If it does not work, you adjust. The cost of the wrong choice is some wasted time. The cost of delaying the choice is also wasted time, often more of it.

An irreversible decision is one where the cost of being wrong is high and changing course is expensive or impossible. Choosing a database technology for a system that will store years of customer data. Signing a multi-year vendor contract. Laying off a team. Making a public commitment to a delivery date that ties to a partner launch. These decisions deserve careful analysis because the consequences persist long after the decision is made.

Most decisions in an organization are reversible. But most organizations treat them as if they are not. This is one of the primary sources of organizational slowness. Teams deliberate for weeks over choices that could be tested in days. Committees form around decisions that a single person could make in an afternoon. The cost of the deliberation exceeds the cost of being wrong, but nobody calculates that because the cost of deliberation feels like diligence.

Here is a practical test. Before any decision, ask: what happens if we are wrong? If the answer is "we roll it back and try something else," make the decision now. If the answer is "we are locked in for two years and migration will cost six months of engineering time," slow down.

For reversible decisions, optimize for speed. Decide at 70 percent information. Set a timeline for evaluating the result. Be prepared to adjust.

The cost of a wrong reversible decision is almost always less than the cost of delaying a right one.

For irreversible decisions, optimize for quality. Gather more information. Consult more perspectives. Stress-test your assumptions. Accept that the process will be slower, and protect the time to do it well.

There is a useful exercise for building this muscle. For one week, before every decision you participate in, ask yourself: is this a one-way door or a two-way door? A one-way door is hard to walk back through. A two-way door lets you return to where you started. You will be surprised how many decisions that feel permanent are actually two-way doors that have been treated as one-way doors out of habit.

Once a team starts seeing this distinction, the velocity of decision-making increases dramatically. Not because people become less careful, but because they stop spending careful energy on decisions that do not require it.

When Analysis Becomes Avoidance

A platform engineering team at a healthcare technology company was tasked with choosing a new observability stack. Their existing monitoring setup was a patchwork of open-source tools that required constant maintenance. On-call engineers spent more time managing the monitoring system than investigating actual incidents. Everyone agreed the situation was unsustainable.

The tech lead, Omar, assembled a working group. They inventoried the current tools. They defined evaluation criteria. They created a weighted scoring matrix. They identified six candidate platforms. They requested demos from all six vendors. They ran two weeks of proof-of-concept testing with three finalists. They documented the results in a 40-page evaluation report.

Then the questions started. Could they test with production traffic instead of synthetic data? Could they extend the POC to include the mobile team's use case? Could they get pricing commitments that accounted for projected growth over three years? Could they benchmark the alerting latency under peak load conditions?

Each question was reasonable. Each one extended the timeline by one to two weeks. Omar scheduled additional POC phases, additional vendor calls, additional stakeholder reviews. The evaluation that was supposed to take four weeks stretched to four months.

During those four months, three things happened. The on-call team continued to suffer. Two experienced engineers cited the monitoring burden as a factor in their decisions to leave the company. And one of the three finalist vendors released a major update that invalidated a portion of the POC results, prompting a discussion about whether to re-run the tests.

Omar's CTO finally intervened. She asked one question: "If you had to choose today, which one would you pick?"

Omar answered immediately. He did not hesitate. He named the platform he had favored since week three of the evaluation.

She asked the follow-up: "What information from the last three months changed your ranking?"

He thought about it. Nothing had. The additional analysis had confirmed his initial assessment without altering it. He had spent three months increasing his confidence from 75 percent to 85 percent. During that time, the team lost two engineers, the on-call burden worsened, and the winning vendor's pricing had actually increased because the company missed the end-of-quarter discount that had been available during the original timeline.

The decision was made that afternoon. The platform was deployed within six weeks. It worked. Not perfectly. There were integration challenges and a learning curve. But the monitoring burden dropped by 70 percent in the first quarter, and the on-call team went from dreading their rotation to actually being able to focus on incident response.

Omar's mistake was not that he was thorough. Thoroughness is a virtue. His mistake was that he did not distinguish between the analysis that informed the decision and the analysis that delayed it. The first four weeks produced clarity. The next twelve produced comfort. And comfort is not worth two engineers and a quarter of the team's morale.

This pattern is everywhere. Technical leaders who are excellent analysts often struggle with decision commitment because their analytical strength gives them an infinite supply of useful questions to investigate. Every question has value. But past a certain point, the cumulative cost of the questions exceeds the cumulative value of the answers. Recognizing that inflection point is one of the most important skills a technical leader can develop.

What Most Developers Get Wrong About Decisions

Three misconceptions keep engineers from becoming effective decision-makers.

The first is believing that more information always leads to better decisions. It does not. Information has diminishing returns. The first 50 percent of information transforms your understanding of the problem. The next 20 percent refines it. The 20 percent after that adjusts details. The final 10 percent is noise that feels like signal. Most teams spend disproportionate effort pursuing the last 30 percent, which rarely changes the direction of the decision. It only makes them feel more justified in the direction they were already heading.

The second is conflating confidence with accuracy. Feeling certain about a decision does not make it correct. Feeling uncertain about a decision does not make it wrong. Some of the best decisions you will ever make will feel uncomfortable when you make them. Some of the worst decisions you will ever make will feel obvious. Confidence is an emotional state, not an epistemic one. The engineer who refuses to decide until they feel confident is using the wrong metric. The right metric is: do I have enough information to form a defensible position? If yes, decide, regardless of how you feel about it.

The third is treating every decision as equally important. This is the most common mistake and the most expensive. Not every decision deserves a working group, an evaluation matrix, and a month of analysis. The choice of which monitoring tool to use for a new internal service does not warrant the same process as the choice of which cloud provider to commit to for the next five years. But many organizations apply the same decision-making overhead to both because they have not built the habit of calibrating effort to stakes.

Here is a diagnostic. Look at the last five decisions your team made. How long did each one take? Now ask: could the outcome have been meaningfully different if the decision had been made in half the time? If the answer is no for most of them, your team has a decision-speed problem, not a decision-quality problem.

The Courage to Decide and Be Wrong

There is one more dimension to decision-making under uncertainty that no framework can fully capture. It is the willingness to be wrong.

Most engineers build their professional identity around being right. Being the person who sees the flaw in the design. Being the person who catches the bug before production. Being the person whose technical judgment is consistently sound.

That identity becomes a liability when you move into leadership. Because leadership requires making calls when you cannot be sure you are right. And sometimes you will not be.

The developers who struggle with this try to hedge every decision. They present options instead of recommendations. They use language like "it depends" and "we could go either way." They avoid committing to a direction because committing means being accountable for the outcome.

The developers who thrive in leadership do something different. They form a position, state it clearly, explain their reasoning, and own the consequences. When they are wrong, they acknowledge it, learn from it, and adjust. They do not pretend they were right all along. They do not blame the data or the team. They say: "I made this call, it did not work, here is what I learned, here is what I would do differently."

That kind of transparency builds trust faster than being right ever could. Because people do not follow leaders who are never wrong. They follow leaders who are honest about when they are.

The ability to decide, act, learn, and adapt is more valuable than the ability to analyze endlessly and never commit. Organizations do not need perfect decision-makers. They need people who can move things forward despite incomplete information and take responsibility for the results.

That is what leadership looks like. Not certainty. Judgment, transparency, and the willingness to be accountable.

What to Do Monday Morning

Make one decision faster this week. Just one.

Look at the decisions currently pending on your team. There is almost certainly at least one that has been lingering because nobody has committed to a direction. Maybe it is which library to use for a new feature. Maybe it is how to structure the API for an upcoming integration. Maybe it is whether to refactor a module now or after the next release.

Pick the one that is reversible. Apply the 70% Rule. Ask yourself: do I have 70 percent of the information I need? If yes, form a recommendation and present it. Not as an option among options. As a recommendation with reasoning.

Frame it like this: "I recommend we go with [choice], because [two to three reasons]. The main risk is [risk], but this is a reversible decision, so if we are wrong, we can adjust with [low cost]. The cost of delaying is [what happens if we wait another two weeks]."

That framing does four things. It makes a clear recommendation, which moves the conversation from analysis to action. It shows your reasoning, which builds trust. It names the risk honestly, which demonstrates judgment. And it quantifies the cost of delay, which creates urgency without creating panic.

After the decision is made, set a date to evaluate the outcome. Not an open-ended check-in. A specific date with specific criteria. "In two weeks, we will look at [metric] and decide whether this is working." This creates a feedback loop that turns the decision into a learning opportunity. If the decision was right, you have confirmation. If it was wrong, you catch it early and adjust. Either way, you have real data instead of hypothetical analysis.

Do this once. See what happens. See how it feels to move something forward instead of waiting for more information. Then do it again the following week. Over the course of a month, you will develop a calibration for how much information is actually necessary for different types of decisions. That calibration is worth more than any framework.

The point is not to be impulsive. The point is to recognize that the discipline of deciding is a skill that atrophies without use. Every decision you delay trains your instinct toward caution. Every decision you make, evaluate, and learn from trains your instinct toward judgment. The engineers who develop that judgment early are the ones who get trusted with the decisions that actually matter.

Checklist: Are You Waiting for Certainty?

Before moving to the next chapter, run through this honestly.

Is there a decision on your team right now that has been pending for more than two weeks? If yes, ask whether the delay is producing new information or just producing comfort. If the direction has not changed since week one, you are paying for confidence, not clarity.

When you present options to stakeholders, do you include a recommendation, or do you present the options and wait for someone else to choose? If you wait, you are operating as an analyst, not a decision-maker. The room is looking for someone to take a position.

Can you distinguish between the reversible and irreversible decisions on your current roadmap? If you cannot, you are likely applying the same deliberation speed to everything, which means you are too slow on the small things and possibly too fast on the big ones.

When was the last time you made a decision that turned out to be wrong? If you cannot remember, you are either extraordinarily lucky or you are not making enough decisions. People who decide frequently are wrong sometimes. That is how the math works. If you are never wrong, you are probably not deciding.

Do you know the cost of delay for your current pending decisions? Not the risk of deciding wrong. The cost of not deciding at all. If you have never calculated that cost, you are missing half the equation.

When you make a decision, do you set a specific date and criteria for evaluating the outcome? If not, your decisions float without feedback. You never learn whether your judgment was sound because you never close the loop.

After a decision goes wrong, do you analyze what happened and share the learning with the team, or do you move on quietly? If the latter, you are wasting the most valuable byproduct of being wrong. The learning from a bad decision, openly shared, improves the next ten decisions.

Has anyone on your team ever said "we should have decided this weeks ago"? If yes, and they were right, that is a signal that your decision-making process is calibrated for more certainty than the situation requires.

If more than half of these pointed toward waiting for certainty, that is not a character flaw. It is an engineering instinct applied to the wrong domain. The compiler rewards certainty. Organizations reward movement. The gap between those two reward systems is where most engineers get stuck.

Closing that gap starts with one faster decision, made this week, on something that can be undone.

The next chapter explores the skill that turns good decisions into organizational momentum: building influence without authority, and how to lead when you are not in charge.

CHAPTER 7

Building Influence Without Authority

The Person Nobody Invited

There is a meeting happening right now, somewhere in your organization, where the direction of your product is being shaped. A roadmap is being revised. A trade-off is being made between two competing priorities. A hiring plan is being adjusted. A technical investment is being quietly deprioritized.

You were not invited.

This is not because anyone is trying to exclude you. It is because nobody thought of you. The people in that room are the people who have established themselves as relevant to the conversation. They have built the kind of presence where their absence would feel like a gap.

Most developers never reach that level. They do excellent technical work, earn respect within their team, and remain invisible to the people making the decisions that shape what their team builds. They are trusted to execute. They are not consulted on direction.

The gap between being trusted to execute and being consulted on direction is influence. And understanding how influence actually works inside organizations is one of the most important things a developer can learn on the path to leadership.

Influence vs Authority

Most developers conflate influence with authority. They assume that the people who shape decisions are the ones with the title and the org chart position. The VP makes the call. The director sets the roadmap. The manager assigns the work.

That is the formal structure. It is not how decisions actually get made.

In every organization, there is a shadow structure that runs alongside the org chart. It is the network of people whose opinions carry weight regardless of their title. The staff engineer whose architectural guidance is treated as near-mandatory. The product manager whose instinct about users is trusted more than any dashboard. The designer whose framing of a problem consistently becomes the team's default lens. The senior developer whose quiet "I do not think that will work" in a planning meeting causes the entire room to pause.

None of these people have authority over the decision. They all have influence over it.

Authority is positional. You get it when someone above you grants it. Influence is earned. You build it through a track record of being right about things that matter, communicated in a way that other people can act on.

For developers, this distinction is critical. You do not need to become a manager to have influence. You do not need to wait for a promotion. You can start building influence from wherever you are, right now, by changing how you engage with the people and decisions around you.

The developers who understand this advance faster than those who wait for authority to be handed to them. Because by the time the title arrives, they have already been operating at that level for months.

The Influence Triangle

Influence is not a single quality. It is the intersection of three forces that reinforce each other. When all three are present, people listen, trust, and act on what you say. When any one is missing, your impact collapses regardless of how strong the other two are.

The first force is Credibility. This is the foundation. Do people believe you know what you are talking about? Credibility in engineering starts with technical competence, but it does not end there. The developer who writes excellent code has credibility with other developers. The developer who also understands the business context, the customer impact, and the organizational constraints has credibility with product managers, designers, and executives. Credibility is audience-specific. You can have deep credibility with your engineering team and zero credibility with the product organization if you have never demonstrated that you understand their world.

Credibility is built through demonstrated judgment, not through volume of opinion. The engineer who speaks three times in a quarter but each time surfaces something nobody else had considered builds more credibility than the engineer who has an opinion on everything. The key to credibility is not being heard often. It is being right when it matters. And over time, the distinction between those two patterns becomes obvious to everyone in the room.

The second force is Clarity. Can people understand what you are saying and act on it? Many technically brilliant engineers have strong credibility but weak clarity. They know the right answer. They cannot communicate it in a way that moves people. Their explanations are too long, too detailed, too pitched at the wrong level. The room respects their knowledge but cannot extract a decision from their input.

Clarity is not about simplifying. It is about structuring your communication so the audience can act on it. A clear recommendation has three parts: what you think should happen, why, and what the trade-off is. That is it. If someone wants the deeper analysis, they will ask. Most people in most meetings do not want the deeper analysis. They want to know what you think and why, delivered in under sixty seconds. The engineers who can do that consistently become the people the room turns to when a decision needs to be made.

The third force is Consistency. Do people trust that you will follow through, that your positions are stable, and that your judgment is reliable over time? An engineer who is brilliant and clear but unpredictable does not build influence. If you change your recommendation based on who is in the room, people stop trusting your judgment. If you raise concerns but never follow up on them, people stop taking your concerns seriously. If you commit to doing something and then do not do it, every future commitment is discounted.

Consistency is the slowest force to build and the fastest to destroy. It takes months of reliable behavior to establish a reputation for consistency. It takes one broken commitment or one visible flip-flop to damage it. The good news is that consistency does not require being right all the time. It requires being honest all the time. The engineer who says "I recommended this approach, it did not work, and here is what I learned" maintains their consistency because the pattern people are tracking is not correctness. It is integrity.

All three forces of the Influence Triangle must be present simultaneously. Credibility without clarity means people trust your expertise but cannot act on it. Clarity without credibility means your communication is crisp but nobody believes it. Credibility and clarity without consistency means people listen to you in the moment but do not count on you over time. The engineers who build all three become the people organizations cannot function without, regardless of their title.

The Engineer Nobody Heard

Two senior engineers at a logistics platform both identified the same problem. The company's routing algorithm was hitting performance limits as the customer base grew. During peak hours, route calculations that should take milliseconds were taking seconds. The customer experience was degrading. The operations team was getting complaints. Everyone agreed something needed to change.

The first engineer, Tomasz, had been at the company for three years. He was technically excellent. He had written most of the original routing engine. He understood the problem better than anyone. In a planning meeting with product and engineering leadership, he presented his analysis.

He opened with the technical details. He explained the computational complexity of the current algorithm. He walked through the profiling data showing where the bottleneck occurred. He described three possible optimization approaches, each with different performance characteristics. He showed benchmarks from his prototype. His analysis was thorough, accurate, and rigorous.

The product director asked: "So which one should we do?"

Tomasz said it depended on the company's growth projections, which he did not have access to. He said any of the three approaches would improve performance, but the right choice depended on whether the company expected to double its route volume in six months or two years. He suggested the product team provide those projections so he could finalize his recommendation.

The room thanked him. The product director said they would circle back. Two months later, nothing had happened. The routing performance continued to degrade. Tomasz was frustrated. He had given them everything they needed. Why was nobody acting on it?

Here is what Tomasz got wrong. His credibility was high. He had deep expertise. But his clarity was low. He presented three options without a recommendation, which forced the decision-makers to do his synthesis for him. And his consistency was untested, because he delivered the analysis and waited for someone else to act on it rather than driving the outcome.

In the Influence Triangle, he had one leg. Not enough to stand on.

The second engineer, Amara, had been at the company for eighteen months. She had less institutional knowledge than Tomasz but had spent her first year building relationships across engineering and product. She understood the routing problem at a technical level, though not as deeply as Tomasz. She also understood the business context because she had made a habit of reading the quarterly business reviews and talking to the customer success team.

When Amara addressed the same problem, she did not wait for a planning meeting. She wrote a one-page document and shared it with the engineering director and the product director a week before the next planning session. The document had three sections.

The first section described the business impact. Route calculation delays were causing a measurable increase in delivery completion times, which directly affected the company's SLA commitments. Two enterprise customers had flagged the issue in their quarterly reviews. The cost of inaction was quantifiable.

The second section described the recommended approach. Not three options. One recommendation, with the reasoning. She chose the approach that best matched the company's stated growth plan, which she had found in the last board deck that the CEO had shared at an all-hands. She acknowledged the trade-offs and named them explicitly.

The third section described what she needed to move forward. Two engineers for four weeks. A commitment from the product team to defer one medium-priority feature to make room. A checkpoint at the two-week mark to evaluate progress.

In the planning meeting, the product director referenced Amara's document. The engineering director had already reviewed it and agreed with the approach. The decision was made in ten minutes. The project shipped six weeks later. Route performance improved by a factor of eight.

Amara's technical analysis was less detailed than Tomasz's. Her understanding of the algorithm was shallower. But she operated across all three sides of the Influence Triangle. She had credibility because she connected the technical problem to business outcomes. She had clarity because she made a single recommendation with explicit reasoning. She had consistency because she did not drop the document and wait. She followed up, she drove the timeline, and she delivered the result.

Tomasz had the right answer. Amara had influence. In organizations, influence wins.

How Decisions Actually Get Made

If you want to influence decisions, you need to understand how decisions actually happen inside organizations. The formal process looks clean. There is a proposal, a review, a decision, and an execution plan. Inputs go in, a decision comes out.

The reality is much messier.

Most organizational decisions are made in pieces, over time, through a series of informal conversations that happen before the formal meeting ever takes place. By the time a decision reaches the meeting room, it is often already made. The meeting is the ratification, not the deliberation.

This means that if you want to influence a decision, you need to be part of the conversations that happen before the meeting. The hallway discussion. The Slack thread. The one-on-one where a director thinks out loud about their priorities. The design review where the real constraints surface for the first time.

Developers who only show up for the formal process are always too late. The positions have already been formed. The alliances have already been built. The framing has already been set. Trying to change the direction of a decision in the official meeting is like trying to redirect a river after it has already carved its path.

This is not political maneuvering. It is organizational awareness. Understanding where and when decisions actually take shape, and making sure your perspective is part of the conversation at the right moment.

There are three phases to every significant organizational decision, and your influence strategy should be different in each one.

The first phase is formation. This is when the problem is being defined and the initial framing is taking shape. This is the highest-leverage moment for influence because the framing determines what solutions are even considered. If the problem is framed as "we need a faster database," the solution space is narrow. If the problem is framed as "our read performance is degrading because of how we modeled the data three years ago," the solution space is much wider. The engineer who contributes to the framing shapes everything that follows.

The second phase is evaluation. This is when options are being compared and trade-offs are being weighed. Your influence in this phase depends on whether you can surface information that changes the calculus. Data the room does not have. Risks the room has not considered. Alternatives the room has not imagined. The engineer who brings new information during evaluation shifts the outcome.

The third phase is commitment. This is when the decision crystallizes and people align around a direction. Your influence in this phase is about helping the decision stick. Volunteering to own a piece of the execution. Publicly supporting the chosen direction, even if it was not your preferred option. Making it easy for the decision-maker to feel confident that the team is aligned. The engineer who supports decisions well, even imperfect ones, builds trust that increases their influence in the next cycle.

Most developers only participate in the second phase, and only when invited. The ones who participate in all three become indispensable.

What Most Developers Misunderstand About Influence

Three misconceptions prevent engineers from building the influence their expertise warrants.

The first is thinking influence is about being persuasive. It is not. Persuasion is a single interaction. Influence is a reputation. You do not build influence by winning arguments. You build it by being the person whose judgment people trust because it has been consistently sound over time. The engineer who wins every debate but is seen as combative has less influence than the engineer who loses some debates gracefully but is seen as thoughtful and reliable. Influence is not about the moment. It is about the pattern.

The second is thinking influence requires visibility. Many engineers believe that building influence means presenting at all-hands meetings, writing blog posts, or being active on Slack. Visibility helps, but it is not influence. Influence is when people change their behavior based on your input. You can be highly visible and have zero influence if people consume your content but do not act on it. You can be barely visible and have enormous influence if the six people you interact with regularly trust your judgment and propagate your thinking to their teams. Influence is measured by action, not by audience.

The third is thinking influence is a fixed resource that you either have or do not. Influence is contextual. You can have enormous influence on architecture decisions and zero influence on hiring decisions. You can have strong influence within your team and no influence with the product organization. The misconception that influence is a global attribute leads engineers to either overestimate their reach or underestimate their potential. The reality is that influence is built domain by domain, relationship by relationship. You start where your credibility is strongest and expand outward.

Understanding these misconceptions clears the path to building influence deliberately. It is not about personality. It is not about politics. It is about credibility, clarity, and consistency, applied in the right contexts, with the right people, over enough time for the pattern to become visible.

Stakeholder Management as Influence Architecture

The phrase "stakeholder management" sounds corporate. Most developers hear it and think of something that product managers do. But once you start operating beyond your immediate team, stakeholder management becomes the practical infrastructure of influence.

A stakeholder is anyone who has a vested interest in the outcome of your work. Your engineering manager, obviously. But also the product manager counting on your team's delivery. The designer whose work depends on your technical feasibility assessment. The director tracking your project as part of a larger initiative. The customer success team that will support whatever you ship. The other engineering team whose roadmap intersects with yours.

Each of these people has different priorities, different concerns, and different definitions of success. The product manager cares about the timeline. The designer cares about the user experience. The director cares about strategic alignment. The support team cares about reliability and documentation.

Most developers focus exclusively on the technical quality of their work and assume the rest will take care of itself. It does not. A technically excellent project that surprises stakeholders with its timeline, confuses them with its scope, or fails to meet their unstated expectations will be perceived as a failure, regardless of the code quality.

Managing stakeholders does not mean telling them what they want to hear. It means understanding what they care about and keeping them informed in terms they can act on. It means surfacing risks early instead of hoping they resolve themselves. It means translating progress into language that maps to their priorities.

"We completed the API refactor" means nothing to a product manager. "We are on track for the feature launch date, and the refactor reduced our estimated integration time by a week" means everything.

Here is a practical starting point. For every project you work on, identify the three people outside your immediate team who care most about the outcome. Learn what they care about. Send them a brief update once a week that answers their specific concerns. "The integration is on track and we reduced the estimated downtime from four hours to ninety minutes" tells the ops lead exactly what they need to know. "Sprint velocity is on target" tells them nothing.

This takes ten minutes per stakeholder per week. The return is disproportionate. Within a few months, those stakeholders will start advocating for you and your team in conversations you are not part of. They become amplifiers of your influence, not because you asked them to, but because you made their job easier.

Aligning Engineering, Product, and Leadership

One of the most common failure modes in technology organizations is misalignment between engineering, product, and executive leadership. Each group has a different view of reality, and they rarely compare notes in a way that surfaces the gaps.

Product sees the market opportunity and the customer demand. They want features, and they want them fast. Engineering sees the technical constraints, the debt, and the system fragility that product does not understand. They want time to build things properly. Leadership sees the financial targets and the competitive landscape. They want predictable delivery and measurable results.

All three perspectives are valid. The problem is that each group advocates for their own view without translating it into terms the other groups can evaluate.

The developer who can bridge these perspectives is extraordinarily valuable. They can explain to product why a particular feature request is more expensive than it appears, and propose an alternative that delivers eighty percent of the value at thirty percent of the cost. They can explain to leadership why a reliability investment that produces no visible features will actually accelerate feature delivery in the next quarter. They can explain to the engineering team why a seemingly arbitrary business deadline actually matters and what is at stake if it slips.

This is the translation work from Chapter 3, applied at the organizational level. It is not about being a mediator. It is about being the person who understands all three perspectives well enough to find the alignment point that serves everyone.

Most organizations do not have enough of these people. The ones who can hold the technical, product, and business perspectives simultaneously and communicate across all three are rare. When you find someone who can do it, they tend to rise quickly. Not because they are political. Because they make everyone around them more effective.

This is a skill you can practice deliberately. The next time you are in a cross-functional meeting, try this exercise. For every point raised, mentally translate it into the other two perspectives. When product says "we need this feature by Q3," ask yourself: what does engineering need to know to evaluate that, and what does leadership need to know to support it? The ability to hold all three frames simultaneously does not come naturally. But it can be developed through repetition.

What to Do Monday Morning

You need two habits to build trust fast. Start both this week.

The first habit: share your thinking before it is asked for. Most developers wait to be consulted. They have opinions about the roadmap, the architecture direction, the team's process, and the product strategy. Those opinions stay in their heads until someone invites them to speak.

Stop waiting. This week, write a short document, three paragraphs maximum, about something you believe the team should do differently. It could be a technical risk nobody is tracking. A process that is slowing the team down. An alternative approach to a planned feature that would deliver better results. Share it with your engineering lead or your product manager with a single question: "I have been thinking about this. Would it be useful for me to present it to the team?"

You are not asking for permission to have an opinion. You are demonstrating that you think beyond your own tasks and offering your judgment for the team's benefit. Some of the time, the answer will be "not now." But the fact that you proactively shared your thinking registers. Over time, it changes your reputation from "strong executor" to "someone who sees the bigger picture." That shift in reputation is the inflection point where influence begins.

The second habit: close the loop on everything. When someone asks for your input, follow up after the decision is made. When you raise a concern, check back in a week to see if it was addressed. When you commit to investigating something, report back even if the answer is "I looked into it and there is nothing to worry about."

Most engineers let threads drop. They answer the question and move on. They raise the risk and forget about it. They investigate and never share the result. Each dropped thread is a small erosion of consistency. Each closed loop is a small deposit into trust. Over a month, the difference compounds. The engineer who closes every loop becomes the engineer people rely on. And reliance is the precondition for influence.

These two habits together activate the Influence Triangle. Sharing your thinking proactively builds credibility and clarity. Closing the loop builds consistency. Within a quarter, the compounding effect is visible. People seek your input. They forward your documents. They include you in conversations that used to happen without you.

Checklist: Do People Act on What You Say?

Before moving to the next chapter, run through this honestly.

When you make a recommendation in a meeting, does the room move in that direction, or does the conversation continue as if you had not spoken? If your contributions do not change the trajectory of discussions, your influence is lower than your expertise warrants. The gap is usually clarity or timing, not credibility.

In the last month, has anyone outside your immediate team sought your opinion on a decision? If not, your influence radius is smaller than it could be. People seek opinions from people they trust. If they are not seeking yours, either they do not know what you know, or your track record has not reached them.

Do the people you work with most closely know your perspective on the team's biggest challenges before you tell them? If yes, your thinking is being anticipated, which means it is being trusted. If no, you are operating as a surprise rather than a resource.

When you disagree with a decision, do you voice it early in the process or only after the decision is made? If after, you are providing commentary instead of providing input. Commentary does not build influence. Input does.

Can you name three people outside your team who would describe you as someone whose judgment they trust? If not, your influence infrastructure is too narrow. Start with stakeholder updates this week.

After you share a document, an analysis, or a recommendation, do you follow up to see what happened? If you share and forget, you are building credibility but not consistency. The follow-up is what closes the triangle.

When a decision you advocated for turns out to be wrong, do you acknowledge it openly? If not, you are protecting your credibility at the expense of your consistency. Owning a mistake publicly is the fastest way to build trust, because people learn that you value honesty over being right.

Do people forward your messages or reference your documents in conversations you are not part of? If yes, your influence is compounding. If no, your communication may be clear to the people in the room but not structured in a way that travels.

If more than half of these pointed toward low influence, that is not a judgment of your value. It is information about the gap between your expertise and your impact. That gap is closable. It does not require a personality change. It requires the Influence Triangle: credibility built through demonstrated judgment, clarity built through structured communication, and consistency built through relentless follow-through. All three are skills. All three improve with practice. And the compounding starts faster than most engineers expect.

The next chapter shifts from influence to infrastructure: the practical toolkit of leadership, and the specific skills, processes, and habits that turn strategic thinking into organizational results.

CHAPTER 8

The Leadership Toolkit

From Principles to Practice

The previous chapters laid out the mindset shifts that developers need to make on the path to leadership. Thinking strategically. Communicating across audiences. Managing people. Reasoning about systems. Making decisions under uncertainty. Building influence.

Those ideas are useful. But ideas without tools are just intentions.

This chapter is different. It is the practical chapter. The one you come back to when you are sitting in front of a real problem and need something concrete to reach for. Every tool here is something you can start using this week. None of them require permission, budget, or a new title.

The best developer-leaders do not rely on instinct alone. They build habits and systems that make good judgment repeatable. They create structures that make their thinking visible to others. They use lightweight processes that scale without becoming bureaucracy.

That is what a leadership toolkit is. Not a checklist. A set of practices that help you operate consistently at a level above pure execution.

What Most Developers Lack When They Step into Leadership

The gap is not knowledge. Most developers who step into leadership roles have read the books, attended the talks, and absorbed the principles. They understand that communication matters, that delegation is important, that strategic thinking is valuable. The gap is systems.

Knowledge tells you what to do. Systems make you do it consistently.

Think about how you became a good developer. You did not just learn syntax and algorithms. You built systems. You learned to write tests before shipping. You created a code review habit. You developed a debugging process that you follow every time something breaks. You built linting rules, CI pipelines, and deployment checklists. These systems turned your knowledge into repeatable performance. Without them, your technical quality would be inconsistent, dependent on your energy level, your mood, and whether you remembered to check the edge cases.

Leadership has the same problem. The developer who knows they should give feedback but has no system for it will give feedback sporadically, usually when frustration forces it. The developer who knows they should communicate with stakeholders but has no system for it will communicate when something goes wrong, which is the worst possible time. The developer who knows they should delegate but has no system for it will delegate inconsistently, sometimes micromanaging and sometimes disappearing entirely.

Most leadership failures are not failures of judgment. They are failures of consistency. And consistency comes from systems, not from willpower.

The three tools in this chapter are not the only tools you will ever need. But they are the three that produce the most immediate impact for engineers stepping into leadership. A decision log creates institutional memory. A stakeholder map creates organizational awareness. Delegation levels create scalable impact. Together, they form the minimum viable infrastructure of a leadership practice.

Tool One: The Decision Log

Most teams make dozens of significant decisions every quarter and document almost none of them. Three months later, nobody remembers why a particular approach was chosen, what alternatives were considered, or what assumptions the decision was based on.

This creates two problems. First, the team relitigates the same decisions over and over because there is no record of the original reasoning. Second, when a decision turns out to be wrong, there is no way to trace it back to the faulty assumption and learn from it.

A decision log solves both problems. It is simple. For every significant decision, you write down five things: the date, what was decided, what alternatives were considered, why this option was chosen, and what assumptions it depends on.

That is it. A few sentences per entry. Five minutes.

Here is what an actual entry looks like. "March 14, 2026. Decided to use PostgreSQL for the new reporting service instead of the existing MongoDB cluster. Alternatives considered: MongoDB (existing), DynamoDB (managed), PostgreSQL (new). Chose PostgreSQL because the reporting queries are heavily relational and the current MongoDB schema requires expensive aggregation pipelines that are already hitting performance limits. Assumptions: reporting query patterns will remain primarily relational; the team can absorb the operational overhead of a new database within the existing on-call rotation; traffic will not exceed 5,000 queries per hour for the first year."

That entry took four minutes to write. It will save four hours the first time someone asks "why did we add another database?" It will save more than that the first time the assumption about query patterns or traffic volume changes and the team needs to know which decisions to re-evaluate.

The most important part of a decision log is the assumptions section. Decisions are only as good as the assumptions they rest on. When you write down "we assumed traffic would stay below 5,000 queries per hour," you create a tripwire. The moment that assumption becomes false, you know the decision needs to be revisited. Without the log, you discover the assumption was wrong when the system breaks. With the log, you discover it when someone checks the metrics and cross-references the documented threshold.

There is a secondary benefit that is easy to overlook. The act of writing down your reasoning forces you to clarify your thinking before you commit. When you have to articulate why you chose option A over option B, you sometimes realize that your reasoning does not hold up. The decision log is not just a record. It is a thinking tool.

Start with your own decisions. You do not need the team to adopt it. Keep a personal decision log in a shared document or a wiki page. Within a few months, you will find yourself referencing it constantly. And other people will start asking for it. That is how the practice spreads. Not through mandates. Through demonstrated utility.

Tool Two: The Stakeholder Map

Chapter 7 introduced the concept of stakeholder management. A stakeholder map is the tool that makes it operational.

A stakeholder map answers four questions for every project you work on. Who cares about this work? What specifically do they care about? How informed do they need to be? And how will you keep them informed?

Here is how to build one. At the start of any project that touches more than your own team, take thirty minutes with a blank document. Draw three concentric rings.

The inner ring is your core stakeholders. These are the people who are directly affected by the outcome and who can block or accelerate your progress. Your engineering manager. Your product manager. The tech lead of a team whose API you depend on. These people need frequent, detailed communication. Weekly updates at minimum. Direct conversations when risks surface.

The middle ring is your informed stakeholders. These are people who care about the outcome but are not directly involved in the execution. A director tracking your project as part of a larger initiative. The customer success team that will support whatever you ship. A dependent team that needs to plan around your delivery. These people need periodic updates. Biweekly summaries. A heads-up before anything changes that affects them.

The outer ring is your aware stakeholders. These are people who should know the project exists and what it means but do not need operational detail. Other engineering teams. The executive who approved the budget. The broader product organization. These people need occasional visibility. A launch announcement. A quarterly summary. An invitation to a demo.

For each person in each ring, write one sentence about what they care about most. The VP cares about timeline and budget. The dependent team cares about backward compatibility. Security cares about compliance. Customer success cares about user-facing impact. That sentence determines the content of your communication with them. You are not sending a generic update. You are answering their specific question before they have to ask it.

Then decide the cadence and channel. The VP gets a biweekly email summary. The dependent team gets a technical update in their Slack channel. Security gets a review session before launch. Customer success gets a heads-up two weeks before any user-facing change.

This exercise takes thirty minutes. It prevents the kind of surprises that derail projects, damage trust, and create the perception that engineering operates in a bubble. The developers who use stakeholder maps consistently earn a reputation for being organized, reliable, and easy to work with. Those are not glamorous qualities. They are the qualities that get you included in the next important initiative.

There is a subtlety to stakeholder mapping that most guides miss. The map is not static. It changes as the project evolves. A stakeholder who was in the outer ring during planning may move to the inner ring during launch if their team is affected by a rollout complication. Review your map every two weeks and adjust. The engineer who maintains an accurate stakeholder map throughout a project operates with a level of organizational awareness that most of their peers do not reach.

Tool Three: Delegation Levels

As your influence grows, you will face a problem that most developers are not prepared for. There is more work than you can do yourself.

The instinct is to work harder. Stay later. Take on more. This is the executor mindset from Chapter 2, and it does not scale. The developer-leader's job is not to do more work. It is to ensure the right work gets done by the right people.

Delegation is where most new leaders fail. They either delegate too little, bottlenecking the team on themselves, or they delegate too much, losing visibility into critical work. The reason is that they think of delegation as binary. Either I do it or someone else does it.

Delegation is not binary. It operates on a spectrum with five levels.

Level one: do it, and I will tell you how. This is for junior team members working on tasks where the approach matters and the cost of a wrong approach is high. You define the method. They execute it. This is the most time-intensive form of delegation and should be used sparingly.

Level two: research it, and recommend an approach. They investigate the problem, evaluate the options, and bring you a recommendation. You make the final decision. This develops their judgment while maintaining quality control. It is the most effective delegation level for growing mid-level engineers.

Level three: decide and tell me before you act. They own the analysis and the recommendation. They tell you the plan before executing. You can redirect if needed, but you are not driving. This works for experienced engineers on moderately important decisions. It builds autonomy while keeping a safety net.

Level four: decide and act, then tell me what you did. They own the decision and the execution. They update you after the fact. You are informed, not involved. This is appropriate for senior engineers on reversible decisions within their domain. It frees up your time while maintaining awareness.

Level five: own it completely. They make the decisions, execute, and handle the consequences. You do not need to be informed unless they choose to share. This is the full autonomy level, appropriate for experienced people on work that is well within their capability. This is where you should aim to get your strongest team members.

The power of this model is that it makes delegation explicit. Instead of vaguely saying "can you handle this?" you say "I would like you to take this at level three. Research the options, decide what you think is best, and tell me the plan before you start implementing." That single sentence sets expectations for both of you. They know how much autonomy they have. You know what visibility to expect.

Most new leaders default to level one or level five with nothing in between. They either micromanage or abdicate. The five-level model gives you the granularity to match the delegation level to the person's experience, the task's importance, and the consequences of a wrong approach.

Over time, your goal should be to move each person up the levels as they grow. Someone who starts at level two on a particular type of work should be at level four within six months if you are developing them well. The trajectory matters more than the starting point.

There is a common fear that delegation will make you less valuable. The opposite is true. The developer who does everything themselves is capped at the output of one person. The developer who effectively delegates multiplies their impact by the number of people they enable. The first person is an excellent individual contributor. The second is a leader. Organizations reward the second because the second makes the organization better, not just the codebase.

Communication Templates

Chapter 3 made the case that communication is a force multiplier. Templates make that multiplier repeatable.

This is not about filling in blanks on a form. It is about having a go-to structure for the types of communication you do most frequently. When you have a structure, you spend less time figuring out how to say something and more time making sure you are saying the right thing.

There are four communication patterns that cover most of what a developer-leader needs.

The first is the status update. Keep it to three elements: what is on track, what is at risk, and what you need from the reader. That is it. No narrative about what you did last week. No comprehensive list of every ticket that was closed. Just the information that allows someone to act.

The second is the technical proposal. Start with the problem you are solving and why it matters. Then state your recommendation. Then explain the alternatives you considered and why you rejected them. Then outline the trade-offs of your recommendation. End with what you need: a decision, feedback, or resources. This structure works whether you are writing a one-page Slack message or a ten-page design document.

The third is the decision request. State the decision that needs to be made. Provide the context necessary to evaluate it. Present the options with their trade-offs. State your recommendation and why. Ask for a decision by a specific date. This format respects the reader's time and makes it easy for them to say yes, no, or ask a clarifying question.

The fourth is the escalation. Describe the situation factually. Explain what you have already tried. State what you need and why you need it from this specific person. Propose a path forward. Escalations are uncomfortable for developers because they feel like admissions of failure. They are not. They are signals of organizational maturity. The developer who escalates early and clearly prevents small problems from becoming big ones.

You do not need to write these out as formal templates. Just internalize the structures. Over time, they become second nature. Your stakeholders will notice that your communications are consistently clear, actionable, and easy to process. That consistency builds trust faster than any individual message ever could.

Creating Visibility Without Self-Promotion

There is a tension that many developers feel acutely. You know that visibility matters for career growth. But self-promotion feels distasteful. You became an engineer because you liked solving problems, not because you liked talking about yourself.

The good news is that visibility does not require self-promotion. It requires making your work and your team's work legible to the rest of the organization.

The distinction matters. Self-promotion says "look at what I did." Visibility says "here is what we learned, here is what we delivered, and here is what it means for the business."

There are practical ways to create visibility that feel natural rather than performative. Write a short summary after every major project launch that explains what was built, what impact it had, and what you learned. Share it in a channel where leadership can see it. Not as a brag. As information that helps the organization understand what engineering is producing.

When you solve a hard problem, write up the approach and share it with the broader engineering team. This positions you as a contributor to the team's collective knowledge, not as someone seeking attention.

When your team ships something significant, highlight the people who made it happen. Credit the specific contributions. Mention the junior developer who figured out the caching strategy. Mention the QA engineer who caught the critical edge case. This makes you visible as a leader while simultaneously making your team visible as well.

The developers who create visibility this way build a reputation without ever appearing to seek one. People start associating them with high-impact work because the evidence is consistently available. When promotion decisions are made, there is a paper trail of contributions that speaks for itself.

The alternative is to do excellent work in silence and hope someone notices. That strategy works occasionally. It fails much more often than developers realize.

What to Do Monday Morning

Pick one tool and apply it this week.

If you have no system for tracking decisions, start a decision log. Open a document. Title it “Decision Log.” Write the first entry about the last significant technical decision your team made. You probably made one in the last two weeks. Write the date, what was decided, what alternatives were considered, why this option won, and what assumptions it rests on. Set a reminder to add an entry after every planning meeting or design review. By the end of the month, you will have a document that already contains more institutional memory than most teams accumulate in a year.

If you have a project that involves anyone outside your immediate team, build a stakeholder map. Take thirty minutes. Draw the three rings. Put names in each ring. Write one sentence about what each person cares about. Decide how and how often you will communicate with them. Then send one proactive update this week to a stakeholder in the middle ring, someone who should be informed but is not directly involved. You will be surprised by how much goodwill a single proactive update generates.

If you are overwhelmed by the volume of work on your plate, assign delegation levels. List the top ten things on your to-do list. Next to each one, write a number from one to five based on the delegation framework. Anything at level one or two that could be at level three or four is a sign that you are doing work someone else should own. Pick one item and explicitly delegate it this week. Tell the person the level. “I would like you to take this at level three. Research the options, recommend an approach, and tell me the plan before you start.” See what happens.

You do not need to adopt all three tools simultaneously. Start with the one that addresses your most immediate pain point. If decisions keep getting relitigated, start the decision log. If stakeholders keep being surprised, build the map. If you are the bottleneck, set delegation levels.

The goal is not to create process. The goal is to create infrastructure that makes your leadership repeatable. A tool you use once is a tactic. A tool you use every week is a system. And systems are what separate the developer who leads effectively once from the developer who leads effectively always.

Checklist: Do You Have a Repeatable System?

Before moving to the next chapter, run through this honestly.

When someone asks why your team made a particular technical decision three months ago, can you point them to a written record, or do you have to reconstruct the reasoning from memory? If from memory, you are losing institutional knowledge every week. A decision log fixes this in five minutes per decision.

Do you know, right now, every person outside your team who has a stake in your current project? If you hesitate, your stakeholder map is incomplete or nonexistent. The stakeholders you forget about are the ones who will be surprised, and surprises damage trust.

For the work you delegated last month, can you name the delegation level for each item? If you cannot, your delegation was implicit, which means expectations were ambiguous. Ambiguous delegation produces either micromanagement or abandonment, depending on your stress level that week.

When you communicate project status, do you have a consistent structure, or does each update require you to figure out the format from scratch? If from scratch, you are spending energy on structure that should be spent on substance. Templates solve this.

After your last project launch, did you share a written summary of the outcome with anyone outside your immediate team? If not, the impact of your work is invisible to the people who make resourcing and promotion decisions. Visibility does not happen automatically. It happens when you create it.

Do your team members know how much autonomy they have on their current work? If they are constantly checking with you on decisions they could make themselves, your delegation model is too restrictive. If they are making decisions that surprise you, your delegation model is too loose. Either way, explicit levels solve it.

Is there a decision on your team right now that you know will be relitigated in the next month because the original reasoning was never written down? If yes, that is your decision log's first entry.

Could you hand your current project to another lead and have them understand the stakeholder landscape, the key decisions, and the delegation structure within an hour? If not, your leadership practice lives in your head, which means it disappears when you go on vacation, change roles, or get pulled into a different priority.

If more than half of these pointed toward "no system," that is the finding. You are leading on instinct, which works when things are calm and fails when things get complex. The tools in this chapter are not overhead. They are load-bearing infrastructure for your leadership practice. Start one this week. Build the habit. Then add the next. Within a quarter, you will operate with a level of consistency and organizational awareness that sets you apart from every developer who is still leading from memory.

The next chapter looks ahead at the landscape that is reshaping everything: the future of technical leadership, and what changes when AI enters the picture.

CHAPTER 9

The Future of Technical Leadership

The Job That Does Not Exist Yet

Five years ago, the role of "AI operator" did not exist. Ten years ago, "DevOps engineer" was a fringe title that most hiring managers did not understand. Twenty years ago, "full-stack developer" was not a category anyone used. The roles we take for granted today were invented in response to shifts that most people did not see coming until they had already happened.

The same thing is happening now. The roles that will define technical leadership in the next decade have not been fully named yet. The job descriptions have not been written. The career ladders have not been formalized. But the work is already being done by the developers who are paying attention.

If you have followed the arc of this book, you have been building toward something specific. Not just a set of skills, but a new way of operating inside technology organizations. Strategic thinking. Clear communication. People leadership. Systems reasoning. Decision-making under uncertainty. Organizational influence. These are not add-ons to a developer's career. They are the foundation of a role that is emerging right now, in real time, at companies that are figuring out what technical leadership looks like when AI handles more and more of the implementation layer.

This chapter is about where that role is heading. Not predictions pulled from a crystal ball. Observations about patterns that are already visible if you know where to look.

What Changes vs What Does Not

Before talking about the future, it is worth separating what is actually changing from what is not. Most commentary on AI and software development conflates the two, which produces either panic or hype depending on the author's disposition. Neither is useful.

What is changing is the implementation layer. AI tools are getting better at writing code, generating tests, debugging, and producing boilerplate at a pace that would have seemed absurd three years ago. A developer working with current AI tools can produce functional code at three to five times the speed they could in 2022. That speed will increase. The gap between specifying what you want and getting a working implementation is collapsing.

What is changing is the review layer. AI can now read code, identify bugs, suggest refactors, and flag security vulnerabilities with increasing reliability. The role of code review is shifting from catching syntax and logic errors to evaluating design decisions and system-level implications that AI does not yet reason about well.

What is changing is the coordination cost. When implementation is faster, more features can be built in the same time. More features mean more integration points, more dependencies, more system complexity. The bottleneck shifts from "can we build it?" to "should we build it, and how does it fit with everything else?" Coordination becomes the scarce resource.

Here is what is not changing.

The need for someone to define the right problem is not changing. AI can solve problems. It cannot identify which problems are worth solving. That requires business context, user understanding, and strategic judgment that no model possesses.

The need for someone to navigate organizational complexity is not changing. AI cannot sit in a meeting with a VP of Product and an engineering director who disagree about priorities and find the framing that aligns them. It cannot read the political dynamics of a restructuring and advise a team on how to position their work. It cannot build the trust relationships that make cross-functional collaboration possible.

The need for someone to make judgment calls under uncertainty is not changing. AI can provide data and analysis. It cannot weigh incommensurable values. It cannot decide whether to prioritize reliability over speed when both matter and resources are fixed. It cannot take responsibility for a decision that might be wrong and own the consequences.

The need for someone to develop other people is not changing. AI can pair-program with a junior developer. It cannot have a one-on-one about their career frustrations. It cannot read the signals that someone is burning out. It cannot give the kind of feedback that changes how a person thinks about their work. Management is fundamentally a human relationship, and no tool changes that.

The developers who understand this distinction have a clear career strategy. Get better at the things that are not changing. Let AI handle more of the things that are. The developers who invest all their energy in becoming faster coders are optimizing for the part of the job that is being automated. The developers who invest in judgment, communication, systems thinking, and people leadership are optimizing for the part that is becoming more valuable.

What Most People Get Wrong About AI

Three misconceptions dominate the conversation about AI and software development. Each one leads to bad career decisions.

The first is that AI will replace developers. It will not. It will replace tasks. The distinction matters. A developer's job is not a single task. It is a bundle of tasks, some of which AI will absorb and some of which it will not touch. The developers whose entire bundle consists of tasks AI can perform are at risk. The developers whose bundle includes judgment, leadership, system design, and cross-functional communication are not at risk. They are in greater demand, because they are the ones who direct the AI and connect its output to organizational outcomes.

The second is that the transition will be sudden. It will not. AI adoption in engineering organizations is gradual, uneven, and shaped by factors that have nothing to do with the technology's capability. Regulatory environments, organizational culture, legacy systems, security concerns, and human inertia all slow adoption. Some companies are operating with AI-augmented workflows today. Others will not adopt them for years. The transition is real, but it is a decade-long shift, not a cliff.

The third is that the right response is to learn AI tools. Learning AI tools is necessary but not sufficient. It is the equivalent of learning a new programming language. Useful, but it does not change your career trajectory. The response that actually matters is to develop the skills that AI tools cannot replicate. Problem definition. Strategic judgment. Communication that bridges technical and business audiences. People management. Organizational navigation. These are the skills that become more valuable as AI becomes more capable, because they are the skills that sit above the layer AI operates on.

The developers who are panicking about AI are focused on the wrong layer. The developers who are ignoring AI are underestimating the pace of change. The developers who are adapting, developing their judgment and leadership skills while incorporating AI into their workflow, are the ones who will thrive.

The Meta-Developer Model

The introduction to this book proposed a term for the kind of developer the future demands. The meta-developer. Now, nine chapters later, that idea should feel less abstract. Let me make it concrete with a model.

The Meta-Developer operates at the intersection of three domains. AI, Systems, and People. Each domain requires a different skill set, and the meta-developer's value comes from integrating all three simultaneously.

The AI domain is about leverage. The meta-developer understands AI tools well enough to direct them effectively. They know how to specify intent precisely, evaluate AI-generated output critically, and design workflows that combine human judgment with machine speed. They are not AI experts. They are expert users of AI, the way a film director is not a camera expert but knows exactly what to point the camera at and how to evaluate the footage.

The Systems domain is about architecture, in the broadest sense. The meta-developer reasons about technical systems, organizational systems, and business systems as a single interconnected whole. They understand how a database choice affects team velocity, how team structure affects system design, and how business model changes create technical constraints. They see the full stack, not just the code stack but the organizational stack that surrounds it.

The People domain is about effectiveness through others. The meta-developer builds teams, develops talent, resolves conflicts, and creates the conditions for high performance. They communicate across audiences. They build influence through clarity and consistency. They make decisions that account for human factors, motivation, trust, and organizational dynamics, not just technical factors.

Most developers are strong in one domain. The best technical architects are strong in Systems. The best engineering managers are strong in People. The developers who are early adopters of AI tools are strong in the AI domain. But operating in only one domain limits your impact.

The meta-developer integrates all three. When they evaluate a new AI tool, they think about how it affects team workflow (People) and system complexity (Systems), not just task speed (AI). When they design a system, they consider who will operate it (People) and how AI tools could change its maintenance profile (AI). When they develop a team member, they think about what skills will remain valuable as AI advances (AI) and how those skills connect to the organization's technical direction (Systems).

This integration is the skill that organizations are most desperate for and least able to find. A developer who is technically strong is common. A developer who is technically strong and a good communicator is less common. A developer who integrates technical depth, organizational awareness, people leadership, and AI fluency is rare. That rarity is your opportunity.

The Evolving Shape of Engineering Organizations

It is not just individual roles that are changing. Entire engineering organizations are being restructured around the new reality.

The traditional engineering organization was optimized for code production. Small teams. Clear ownership. Sprint cycles. Feature delivery. Everything was designed to maximize the throughput of working software from developer keyboards to production environments.

When AI accelerates the production layer, that organizational model starts showing cracks. If a team of five developers can now produce the output that used to take fifteen, the bottleneck shifts from production capacity to decision quality. The organization does not need more developers writing more code. It needs better decisions about what code to write.

This is already happening. Engineering leaders at forward-thinking companies are restructuring teams around outcomes rather than features. They are embedding engineers more deeply in product and business conversations. They are hiring for judgment and communication alongside technical skill. They are creating roles that did not exist two years ago, roles that combine technical depth with strategic thinking, organizational design, and cross-functional leadership.

For developers, this restructuring creates both risk and opportunity. The risk is that roles defined purely by code output become commoditized. As AI tools make individual code production less differentiated, the developer whose only value is writing code will face increasing pressure.

The opportunity is that the roles being created at the top of these restructured organizations are exactly the roles this book prepares you for. Organizations need people who understand technology deeply and can connect it to business outcomes. Who can lead teams through ambiguity. Who can make trade-offs explicit and align diverse stakeholders around a shared direction.

Those roles carry more influence, more compensation, and more resilience to automation than any pure coding role. And there are not nearly enough people qualified to fill them.

Skills That Compound vs Skills That Expire

If you had to divide your professional development time into two categories, the division would be between skills that compound and skills that expire.

Skills that expire are tied to specific implementations. A particular framework. A particular language version. A particular cloud provider's API. These skills are necessary for getting work done today, but their value decays as the landscape shifts. The time you invested in learning jQuery is no longer paying dividends. The same will be true for skills that feel essential right now but are tied to a particular moment in the technology cycle.

Skills that compound are tied to patterns, not implementations. Problem definition gets better with practice and never becomes obsolete. Judgment under uncertainty improves with every decision you make and evaluate. Communication skills translate across every role, every team, and every industry. The ability to design systems that account for human and organizational dynamics applies regardless of what technology stack you are using.

The meta-developer invests disproportionately in compounding skills while maintaining enough implementation skill to stay credible and effective. They learn enough about the latest AI tools to use them well, without making AI tool expertise the center of their professional identity. They keep their technical foundations strong, without letting language-specific mastery become a substitute for the broader skills that drive career growth.

Here is a practical test. Look at the skills you have invested in over the last twelve months. For each one, ask: will this skill be more or less valuable in five years? The ones that will be more valuable are your compounding assets. The ones that will be less valuable are necessary maintenance. Both matter. But the ratio between them determines the trajectory of your career.

What to Do Monday Morning

Audit your skill portfolio. Take fifteen minutes and list the five skills you spent the most time developing in the last six months. For each one, write whether it compounds or expires. If more than three are expiring skills, you have a portfolio imbalance that will cost you over time. Identify one compounding skill from this book, whether it is communication, decision-making, systems thinking, or people management, and commit to one deliberate practice this week.

Then assess your relationship with AI tools. Are you using them daily, occasionally, or not at all? If not daily, start. Not because the tools are perfect. They are not. But because fluency comes from use, and the developers who are fluent with AI tools when the organizational shift arrives will have a structural advantage over those who are still learning. Pick one task you do repeatedly, code review, test writing, documentation, and try running it through an AI tool this week. Evaluate the output critically. Identify where the tool adds value and where it falls short. That evaluation process is itself the skill being developed.

Finally, start a conversation with someone outside engineering about the direction of the business. A product manager. A customer success lead. A sales director. Ask them: what are the biggest challenges you are facing right now? Listen. Do not try to solve anything. Just absorb the context. The meta-developer's advantage is operating at the intersection of technology, business, and people. You build that intersection one conversation at a time.

Checklist: Are You Adapting or Reacting?

Before moving to the final chapter, run through this honestly.

Are you actively using AI tools in your daily workflow, or are you waiting until the organization mandates it? If waiting, you are ceding the learning curve advantage to developers who started earlier. Fluency takes months, and the window for developing it ahead of the majority is closing.

Can you describe how AI is likely to change the work of your specific team in the next two years? If not, you are operating without a map. You do not need perfect predictions. You need a working hypothesis that you update as evidence arrives.

In the last six months, have you invested time in a skill that compounds, such as communication, decision-making, systems thinking, or people leadership? If your entire learning investment went into implementation-level skills, your portfolio is skewed toward the layer that is being automated.

Do you understand what your organization's leadership values most right now, speed, reliability, cost reduction, market expansion? If not, you cannot connect your technical work to the outcomes that matter. That connection is the meta-developer's core function.

When you think about your career in five years, does your vision depend on a specific technology or on a set of capabilities? If the former, your career is fragile. Technologies shift. Capabilities transfer.

Have you had a meaningful conversation with someone outside engineering about business strategy in the last month? If not, your view of the organization is incomplete. The meta-developer operates across domains. That requires understanding domains beyond your own.

Do people in your organization describe you as someone who "gets the big picture," or primarily as someone who "writes great code"? Both are valuable. But if only the latter, your positioning does not reflect the full value you are capable of delivering.

If you disappeared from your organization for a month, would the impact be felt primarily in code output or in decision quality? If code output, your role is still defined by the layer that AI is absorbing. If decision quality, you are already operating as a meta-developer.

If more than half of these pointed toward reacting rather than adapting, that is not a verdict. It is a direction signal. The shift is underway. The window for proactive adaptation is open. The developers who adapt now will define the roles that others will later apply for. The developers who react later will fill those roles on someone else's terms.

CHAPTER 10

The Developer Manifesto

What This Book Was Really About

If you have made it this far, you have spent nine chapters rethinking what it means to be a developer. Not the title. Not the daily tasks. The underlying purpose of the role and where it is heading.

We started with a simple observation. AI is compressing the distance between intent and implementation. The act of writing code, the thing most of us built our careers around, is becoming cheaper and faster every year. That shift is not a threat if you understand what it reveals. The value was never in the typing. It was in the thinking.

This final chapter is not a summary. It is a set of principles. The distilled operating system for the developer who has decided to lead. Not ten pages of explanation. Ten lines you can carry in your head and apply every day.

These principles are not aspirational. They are operational. Each one represents a shift you can make this week. The gap between reading about leadership and practicing it is the gap between understanding and impact.

Here are the principles.

Stop Optimizing for Code. Start Optimizing for Outcomes.

The most dangerous habit a developer can have is measuring their day by how much code they wrote. Code is a means, not an end. The feature that ships perfectly but solves the wrong problem has negative value. It consumed time, created maintenance burden, and distracted from the work that actually mattered.

Before you build, ask: what outcome does this create? Not what does the ticket say. Not what did the product manager request. What change in the world does this produce, and is that change worth the investment?

The developers who ask this question before every project waste less effort, ship fewer things that do not matter, and build a reputation for judgment that no amount of clean code can replicate.

Activity is not progress. Shipping is not impact. Outcomes are impact. Optimize for those.

Clarity Creates Influence.

Your technical judgment is only as valuable as your ability to make it legible to the people who need it. An insight that stays in your head has zero organizational value. A recommendation that nobody understands cannot shape the decision it was meant to improve.

Clear communication is not about being articulate. It is about being precise for the right audience. Say the right thing, to the right person, at the right level, at the right moment.

In a room full of smart people with competing priorities, the person who speaks most clearly wins. Not because they are right more often. Because they are understood more often. And in organizations, being understood is the prerequisite for everything else.

Reduce the distance between what you know and what the other person needs to know. Then stop talking.

The Best Decision Available Now Beats the Perfect Decision Eventually.

Engineers are trained to seek correctness. The compiler rewards it. The test suite demands it. This training becomes a liability when applied to organizational decisions, where correctness is unknowable and delay has a measurable cost.

If you have 70 percent of the information, decide. The remaining 30 percent will cost you weeks to acquire and will rarely change the direction.

The developers who decide at 70 percent and adjust learn faster than the developers who analyze at 95 percent and commit too late.

Separate reversible from irreversible decisions. Move fast on the ones you can undo. Move carefully on the ones you cannot. Most decisions are reversible. Most organizations treat them as if they are not. That mismatch is the primary source of organizational slowness.

Speed on small decisions creates room for rigor on big ones.

Translate, Do Not Explain.

The instinct when someone does not understand you is to explain harder. More detail. More context. More technical depth. This instinct is wrong.

When communication fails, the problem is rarely insufficient information. It is wrong framing. The audience is operating at a different layer than you are. They need business impact, and you are giving them system architecture. They need a decision, and you are giving them an analysis.

Translation is not simplification. It is protocol conversion. The same reality, expressed in the format that the audience can act on. An engineer hears "denormalize the read path." A VP hears "we can cut page load times in half, which directly affects the retention metric you are tracking." Same change. Different protocol. Maximum signal.

Master the translation. The engineer who can speak Code, System, and Business Outcome is the one every organization fights to keep.

Systems Are Bigger Than Software.

The system you are building is not the code. It is the code plus the team that maintains it, the process that deploys it, the organization that funds it, and the incentive structure that shapes all of the above.

A brilliant architecture operated by a burned-out team in a dysfunctional organization will produce mediocre results. A simple architecture operated by a motivated team in a well-aligned organization will produce extraordinary results.

Think in systems. But define the system broadly enough to include the humans. Technical debt is real. Organizational debt is worse. Process debt is invisible until it crushes you.

The developer who can see the full system, from the code to the org chart, is operating at a level that most engineers never reach.

People Are Not Bugs to Fix.

The first instinct of every engineer-turned-manager is to debug their team. Someone is underperforming. Find the root cause. Apply the fix. Move on.

People do not work that way. They are not deterministic. They do not produce stack traces. The same input on Monday produces a different output on Friday. The "fix" that worked for one person fails for the next.

Managing people requires a tolerance for ambiguity that managing systems does not. It requires patience, empathy, and the willingness to sit with problems that do not have clean solutions. It requires giving feedback that lands, not just feedback that is correct. It requires listening more than talking and enabling more than solving.

The engineers who accept this learn to lead. The engineers who keep trying to debug humans frustrate themselves and everyone around them.

Influence Is Earned in Inches.

Nobody wakes up one morning with organizational influence. It accumulates. One clear statement in a meeting. One proactive risk raised before it becomes a crisis. One document that frames a problem better than the hour-long discussion that preceded it. One commitment kept. Then another.

The Influence Triangle has three sides: credibility, clarity, and consistency. Miss any one and the structure collapses. You can be credible but unclear. You can be clear but inconsistent. You can be consistent but lack the credibility to be taken seriously.

Build all three. Be right when it matters. Say it in a way people can act on. Follow through every time. Do this for six months and your organizational reality will look different. Not because you changed your title. Because you changed how people experience working with you.

Influence is not a strategy. It is a pattern of behavior that compounds.

Your Reputation Is Your Résumé.

Titles change. Teams reorganize. Companies merge, shrink, and pivot. The one thing that follows you through every transition is your reputation.

The reputation of being the person who sees clearly. Who communicates honestly. Who delivers reliably. Who makes the people around them better. Who takes responsibility before being asked.

That reputation is built in hundreds of small moments. Every meeting where you contributed something useful. Every time you followed up when you said you would. Every time you gave credit to someone else. Every time you acknowledged a mistake instead of burying it.

Guard it. Build it deliberately. It is the most durable asset you will ever own. Everything else in your career, the promotions, the opportunities, the trust, the scope, flows from it.

Own More Than You Were Assigned.

The developers who become leaders do not wait for responsibility to be granted. They see a gap and they fill it. They notice that a decision is being made without key information and they provide it. They see a process that is hurting the team and they fix it. They recognize that a stakeholder is confused and they reach out.

None of this is in the job description. All of it makes the team and the organization better.

The space between roles is where the biggest problems hide. Nobody owns the communication gap between engineering and product. Nobody owns the onboarding experience that wastes new engineers' first month. Nobody owns the technical decision that three teams are making independently with contradictory assumptions.

Step into that space. Not because you were asked. Because it needs to be done. The title will follow the behavior. The promotion will follow the impact. But the impact always comes first.

Nobody gets promoted into leadership and then starts acting like a leader. They start acting like a leader and then the promotion becomes obvious.

Build for the Long Term.

It is easy to optimize for the next sprint, the next quarter, the next promotion. Short-term thinking is rewarded constantly. Ship the feature. Hit the target. Close the ticket.

Building for the long term means making decisions today that your future self will thank you for. Investing in relationships that will matter three years from now. Building skills that compound rather than depreciate. Choosing the harder conversation now over the comfortable avoidance that creates a bigger problem later.

The skills in this book do not expire. Strategy does not get disrupted by the next AI model. Communication does not become obsolete. People leadership does not depreciate. Systems thinking does not go out of style. These skills get more valuable with every year of experience you apply them.

Every decision you make is an investment. Choose the ones that pay dividends for years, not weeks.

The Next Line of Code

We started this book with a question. If AI can write the code, what exactly is my job?

Now you have the answer.

Your job is everything that surrounds the code. The decisions that determine what gets built. The communication that aligns teams around a shared direction. The leadership that creates the conditions where great work happens. The judgment that separates the right solution from the fast one. The influence that shapes outcomes you never personally implemented.

The code was never the point. The code was always a means to an end. A way to turn ideas into reality, problems into solutions, intentions into outcomes. AI is taking over the means. That leaves you with the end. And the end, it turns out, is where the real value always lived.

The developers who understand this will not just survive the shift. They will define it. They will be the ones building the organizations, setting the strategies, and making the decisions that shape what technology does in the world.

The next line of code may not be yours.

But the next important decision should be.

AFTERWORD

A Note to the Developer Reading This at 2 AM

I know who you are.

You are the person who stayed late to fix the production bug that nobody else could figure out. You are the person who learned a new language over a weekend because the team needed it. You are the person who spent hours writing documentation that nobody asked for because you knew someone would need it later.

You built your career on being reliable, competent, and deeply technical. And for a long time, that was enough.

Now you are reading a book about leadership at two in the morning because something shifted and you can feel it but you are not sure what to do about it. Maybe you got passed over for a promotion and the feedback was vague. Maybe you watched someone with half your technical skill get a leadership role because they could "communicate with stakeholders." Maybe you just looked at the industry news and felt something you had not felt before in your career. Uncertainty.

I wrote this book because I went through the same thing. I spent years defining myself by the quality of my code. I measured my worth by the elegance of my solutions. And then the ground shifted, and I had to figure out what came next.

The answer was not less technical. It was more of everything else. More communication. More strategic thinking. More willingness to sit in ambiguity instead of rushing to a clean solution. More investment in relationships that did not produce immediate, measurable output.

The transition from developer to leader is not a clean upgrade. It is not like learning a new framework where your existing skills transfer neatly. It is more like learning to write with your non-dominant hand while everyone watches. The things that made you successful as a developer, precision, deep focus, independence, comfort with machines over people, some of those things become obstacles in leadership contexts. Not because they are bad qualities. Because they are incomplete.

The hardest part of this transition is not learning the new skills. It is letting go of the identity that says your value comes from the code you produce. That identity served you well. It got you here. But it will not get you where you need to go next.

The good news is that you are not starting from zero. Every complex system you have debugged taught you something about diagnosis and root cause analysis that applies to organizational problems. Every architecture decision you made taught you something about trade-offs and long-term thinking. Every code review where you helped a junior developer taught you something about feedback and mentorship.

You already have more leadership capability than you realize. It is just encoded in technical contexts. This book is about translating it into organizational ones.

I want to be honest about something else. This transition is not for everyone. Some developers will read this book and decide that they want to stay deeply technical. That is a legitimate choice and a respectable career path. The world needs people who go deep. Not everyone needs to lead.

But if you are reading this at two in the morning, I suspect that is not you. I suspect you already know that you want more scope, more influence, more impact. You just did not have a language for it or a map for how to get there.

I also suspect that part of you is afraid you will lose what makes you good. That learning to lead means forgetting how to build. That sitting in meetings means giving up the craft that got you into this industry in the first place.

It does not. The best leaders I have worked with are still builders. They just build at a different scale. Instead of building features, they build teams that build features. Instead of designing systems, they design the conditions under which good systems emerge. The craft does not disappear. It evolves.

Now you do.

The industry is going to keep changing. AI is going to keep compressing the distance between intent and implementation. The roles and expectations that define what it means to be a developer will continue to evolve in ways that nobody can fully predict.

But the skills in this book do not deprecate. The ability to think strategically, communicate clearly, lead people, navigate complexity, make decisions under uncertainty, and build influence across an organization. Those capabilities will be valuable in every version of the future that is worth working toward.

The next line of code might not be yours.

The next important decision still will be.

Now close the laptop and get some sleep. You have work to do on Monday.

ACKNOWLEDGMENTS

Acknowledgments

No book like this gets written alone. There are a lot of people behind these pages, even if their names aren't on the cover.

I've been lucky to work with incredible teams over the years, including at The Washington Post, GoDaddy, and DigiCert. Some of the ideas in this book came from things that worked. A lot of them came from things that didn't. Either way, those experiences shaped how I think about systems, leadership, and what actually matters.

To the people I've worked with day to day, the engineers, product managers, and leaders who challenged ideas, pushed back when it mattered, and made things better than they started, thank you. You know who you are.

To the mentors who gave me honest feedback, even when it wasn't easy to hear, thank you for raising the bar.

To the people who read early drafts and told me when something wasn't landing, or when it didn't feel real, this book is better because of you.

And to my family, thank you for the patience, the support, and for putting up with the nights and weekends this took. It didn't go unnoticed.

APPENDIX A

Chapter Exercises

How to Use These Exercises

Each chapter in this book introduces ideas. Ideas are useful. But ideas without action are entertainment, not development.

The exercises below are designed to be done in your current role, this week, with the team and stakeholders you already work with. They do not require permission, special authority, or a new job title. They require willingness to operate differently for a few hours and then observe what happens.

Do not try to complete all the exercises at once. Pick one per chapter that addresses the gap you identified in the self-assessment. Do it. Reflect on what happened. Then move to the next one.

The exercises are ordered by chapter but they build on each other. The strategic thinking exercises in Chapter 1 make the communication exercises in Chapter 3 more effective. The people leadership exercises in Chapter 4 become easier after you have practiced the decision-making exercises in Chapter 6. Trust the sequence.

Chapter 1: The Changing Landscape

Exercise 1: The Value Audit

Write down the five things you spent the most time on last week. For each one, ask: could an AI tool or a junior developer with AI assistance have done this instead of me? Be brutally honest.

For the items where the answer is yes, ask the follow-up question: what should I have been spending that time on instead? Write down the answer. That gap between what you did and what you should have done is the clearest picture of where your career transition needs to start.

Exercise 2: The Replacement Test

Imagine your company hires a developer with two years less experience than you but full access to the best AI coding tools available. What would they struggle with that you handle easily? Make a list.

Now look at your list. How many items are about writing code, and how many are about everything else? If the list is mostly technical, that is a signal. The technical gap between you and an AI-assisted junior developer is closing faster than you think. The non-technical gap is where your durable advantage lives.

Exercise 3: The Conversation You Are Not Having

Find someone in your organization who works in a role you do not fully understand. A data analyst, a customer success manager, a sales engineer. Ask them for fifteen minutes and ask one question: what does engineering get wrong about what you need?

You will hear things that never appear in tickets or roadmaps. The answers will reveal blind spots in how your team thinks about its work and its users. More importantly, this exercise builds the habit of seeking perspectives outside your technical bubble, which is the first step toward strategic thinking.

Chapter 2: From Executor to Strategist

Exercise 1: The Outcome Rewrite

Take your current sprint or project backlog. Pick three tickets at random. For each one, write a single sentence that describes the business outcome the ticket is meant to produce. Not the technical task. The outcome.

If you cannot write that sentence, you have found a ticket that is being executed without strategic clarity. Bring this observation to your next planning meeting. Not as a complaint. As a question: "What outcome are we trying to produce with this work?"

Exercise 2: The Decision You Are Avoiding

Every developer has at least one decision they have been deferring. A technology that should be replaced. A process that is not working. A conversation that needs to happen. Identify yours.

Write down three things: what the decision is, why you have been avoiding it, and what the cost of continued avoidance is. Then bring it up with the person who needs to hear it this week. You do not need to have the answer. You need to surface the question.

Exercise 3: The Strategy Brief

Write a one-page document that answers these questions about your current project: What problem are we solving? Who are we solving it for? How will we know if we have solved it? What are we choosing not to do and why?

If you cannot answer all four questions clearly, the project lacks strategic clarity. Share the document with your manager or product partner and ask if they agree with your framing. The gap between your understanding and theirs is a conversation that needs to happen before more code gets written.

Chapter 3: Communication as a Force Multiplier

Exercise 1: The Three-Audience Test

Take the last significant technical decision your team made. Write three descriptions of that decision: one for an engineer on another team, one for your product manager, and one for an executive who has five minutes.

Each description should be different. Different level of detail, different framing, different emphasis. If all three sound the same, you are not adjusting for your audience. You are explaining it the way that makes sense to you, which is not the same thing.

Exercise 2: The Silent Meeting

The next time you are in a meeting where you would normally stay quiet, speak up once. Not to show off. To add one specific piece of information, raise one concern, or ask one clarifying question.

After the meeting, note what happened. Did anyone respond to your contribution? Did it change the direction of the conversation? Did you feel uncomfortable? The discomfort is the point. If speaking up in meetings feels risky, that is exactly the muscle you need to build.

Exercise 3: The Written Decision

The next time your team makes a technical decision in a meeting or Slack conversation, write it up afterward. One paragraph: what was decided, why, and what the alternatives were. Share it with the team and ask if anyone remembers it differently.

You will be surprised how often people leave the same conversation with different understandings of what was agreed. This exercise builds the habit of creating written alignment, which is one of the highest-leverage communication skills a technical leader can develop.

Chapter 4: Managing Humans

Exercise 1: The Feedback You Owe Someone

Think of one person you work with who is doing something that is not working. Maybe their code reviews are superficial. Maybe they dominate discussions without listening. Maybe they consistently miss context in their implementations.

Write down what you would say to them if you could be direct without any social consequences. Then edit it until it is honest but constructive. Then deliver it, in person or on a call. Not over Slack. Not in a code review comment. To their face.

This will be uncomfortable. That is the exercise. The skill is not writing the feedback. It is delivering it in a way that the other person can actually hear and act on.

Exercise 2: The Real One-on-One

If you have a one-on-one with a direct report or peer, change the format for one session. Instead of going through status updates, ask three questions: What is the most frustrating part of your current work? What would you change about how the team operates if you could change one thing? Is there something you have been wanting to tell me but have not?

Then stop talking and listen. Do not defend. Do not explain. Do not problem-solve immediately. Just listen and take notes. What you hear will be more valuable than six months of status updates.

Exercise 3: The Difficult Conversation Rehearsal

Identify a difficult conversation you need to have with someone you work with. Write out what you want to say. Then rewrite it three times, each time making it more direct and more specific. Remove every hedge, every qualifier, every "I think maybe" that dilutes the message.

The final version should be clear enough that the person cannot misunderstand your point. You do not have to deliver the most blunt version. But knowing what the direct version looks like gives you a floor of clarity that you can then soften appropriately for the relationship and context.

Chapter 5: Thinking in Systems

Exercise 1: The Second-Order Map

Pick one technical decision that your team made recently. Draw a map of everything it affects beyond the immediate scope. Other teams that consume your API. User workflows that depend on the behavior you changed. Monitoring systems that might alert differently. Deploy pipelines that now have a new dependency.

Most developers stop at first-order effects. This exercise forces you to think one level deeper. If the map surprises you, that is a sign you have been making decisions without full visibility into their consequences.

Exercise 2: The Feature That Should Not Exist

Look at your product backlog and identify one feature or project that you believe should not be built. Not because it is technically hard. Because the expected outcome does not justify the effort, or because it creates dependencies that will cost more than the feature is worth.

Write a one-page argument for why it should be deprioritized. Include the trade-offs and what should be done instead. You do not have to share it immediately. But the act of writing it forces you to practice systems-level thinking and to articulate trade-offs in a way that non-engineers can understand.

Exercise 3: The Dependency Audit

Pick one service or system your team owns and trace every external dependency. Not just the technical ones. Include the teams that consume your output, the teams whose output you consume, the processes that assume your system behaves a certain way, and the people who get paged when it breaks.

Draw it on a whiteboard or a shared document. Then ask your team: did we know about all of these? The dependencies you did not know about are the ones most likely to cause problems during your next major change. This exercise converts invisible risk into visible information.

Chapter 6: Decision-Making Under Uncertainty

Exercise 1: The Decision Log

Start a decision log this week. Every significant decision you make or participate in, write down: what the decision was, what information you had at the time, what information you wished you had, and what you decided.

After two weeks, review the log. Look for patterns. Do you consistently delay decisions waiting for information that never comes? Do you make decisions quickly but miss the same type of consideration repeatedly? The log will reveal your decision-making tendencies more accurately than any personality test.

Exercise 2: The Reversibility Test

Take your current open decisions and sort them into two categories: easily reversible and difficult to reverse. For the easily reversible ones, make them today. Right now. Do not schedule another meeting or gather more data.

The point is to build the habit of matching your decision-making effort to the actual stakes of the decision. Most developers over-invest in reversible decisions because caution is their default mode. Breaking that pattern, even once, changes how you approach decisions going forward.

Exercise 3: The Post-Decision Review

Pick a decision your team made in the last month that produced a clear outcome, good or bad. Write a brief review: what was the decision, what information did you have, what happened, and what would you do differently?

Share it with the team. Not as blame. As learning. The teams that normalize post-decision reviews develop better judgment over time because they create a feedback loop between decisions and outcomes. Most teams have this loop for code through retrospectives and post-mortems. Almost none have it for decisions.

Chapter 7: Building Influence Without Authority

Exercise 1: The Stakeholder Map

Draw a map of the five people who most influence the decisions that affect your work. For each one, answer: what do they care about most? What are they worried about? How do they prefer to receive information? When was the last time you had a direct conversation with them?

If you cannot answer these questions for more than two of the five, your influence network has gaps. Pick one person from the list you do not know well and schedule a twenty-minute conversation this week. Not about a specific issue. About understanding their perspective.

Exercise 2: The Pre-Meeting Move

Before your next important meeting, identify the one person in the room whose support matters most for the outcome you want. Have a brief conversation with them before the meeting. Share your perspective, ask for theirs, and identify any concerns they might raise.

This is not manipulation. It is preparation. Decisions in meetings are shaped by the conversations that happen before them. The developers who understand this have dramatically more influence than the ones who walk in cold and hope their argument is compelling enough.

Exercise 3: The Influence Retrospective

Think about the last three significant decisions that affected your work but that you did not make. For each one, ask: did I have a perspective that should have been part of the discussion? Was I invited to participate? If I was invited, did I speak up? If I was not invited, did I make my perspective known through other channels?

This exercise reveals your influence radius. If you consistently have relevant perspectives that never reach the decision-makers, the problem is not the quality of your thinking. It is the reach of your influence. That is a fixable problem, but only if you see it clearly.

Chapter 8: The Leadership Toolkit

Exercise 1: The Delegation Inventory

List everything on your plate this week. Sort each item into three categories: only I can do this, someone else could do this with guidance, and someone else could do this better than me.

If the first category contains more than 40 percent of your items, you are holding too much. Pick one item from the second category and delegate it this week. Provide clear context about what success looks like, then step back. The goal is not just to free up time. It is to practice the skill of transferring ownership effectively.

Exercise 2: The Visibility Experiment

Write a brief update about something your team accomplished this week and share it with one person outside your team who should know about it. Not a lengthy report. Three to five sentences. What was done, why it mattered, and what comes next.

Do this for three consecutive weeks. Notice what happens. People start asking you questions. They include you in conversations. They think of your team when relevant opportunities arise. Visibility is not bragging. It is the bridge between doing good work and having that work recognized.

Exercise 3: The Process Autopsy

Pick one recurring process your team follows that nobody likes but nobody has changed. A meeting format that wastes time. A review process that adds friction without catching real issues. A reporting cadence that nobody reads.

Write a one-page proposal for replacing it with something better. Include what the current process costs in time and frustration, what you would replace it with, and how you would measure whether the replacement is working. Even if you never submit the proposal, the exercise forces you to think about organizational improvement as a design problem, which is how leaders think about it.

Chapter 9: The Future of Technical Leadership

Exercise 1: The Skills Gap Projection

Imagine your current role three years from now. Write down the three skills you think will be most important for that role in 2029 that are not currently required.

Now assess your current proficiency in each of those three skills. If you are starting from zero in any of them, you have just identified a three-year development priority. The developers who anticipate capability shifts and invest early consistently outperform the ones who wait until the skill becomes a job requirement.

Exercise 2: The AI Collaboration Experiment

Take one task you would normally do yourself and deliberately use AI assistance for 80 percent of it. Then spend your time reviewing, refining, and directing the output rather than producing it from scratch.

Notice what changes. What parts of the task require your judgment? Where does the AI output need human intervention? What did you do with the time you saved? This exercise previews how your role will evolve and reveals whether you are comfortable operating as a director of work rather than a producer of it.

Exercise 3: The Successor Test

Ask yourself: if I left my role tomorrow, who would take over? Could they succeed without me? What would they struggle with?

If the answer to the second question is no, you have a knowledge transfer problem and potentially a single point of failure. List the three things that only you know how to do. Then create documentation or training for at least one of them this month. Leaders who build teams that can function without them are more promotable, not less, because they have demonstrated that they create sustainable capability rather than personal dependency.

Chapter 10: The Developer Leadership Manifesto

Exercise 1: The Personal Manifesto

Write your own leadership manifesto. Not the five principles from this chapter. Your principles. The ones that reflect your specific values, your specific context, and the specific kind of leader you want to become.

Keep it to five principles or fewer. For each one, write a single sentence that explains what it means in practice. Then put it somewhere you will see it every week. A document you review on Monday mornings. A note on your desk. The format does not matter. The regular exposure does.

Exercise 2: The Accountability Partner

Find one person who is also making the transition from developer to leader. Share your self-assessment results and your personal manifesto with them. Set up a monthly check-in where you hold each other accountable for practicing the skills in this book.

Leadership development in isolation is slow and inconsistent. Having someone who will ask you uncomfortable questions about whether you actually did the exercises you committed to makes the difference between reading a book and changing a career.

Exercise 3: The Twelve-Month Letter

Write a letter to yourself, dated twelve months from now. Describe the leader you want to be at that point. Be specific. Not "I want to be better at communication." Instead: "I want to be the person who writes the clearest project briefs on the team. I want to run meetings where decisions get made and everyone leaves knowing what they are responsible for. I want to have built a relationship with at least two stakeholders outside engineering who trust my judgment."

Seal the letter or save it somewhere you will not see it daily. Set a calendar reminder to open it in twelve months. When you read it again, the gap between who you described and who you have become will be the most honest assessment of your growth you will ever receive. The exercise works because it forces you to define success in concrete, behavioral terms rather than vague aspirations.

APPENDIX B

Your First 90 Days

Why Ninety Days

You have read the chapters. You have done the self-assessment. You know which dimensions need work. The question now is how to translate all of that into actual behavioral change without burning out, losing momentum, or reverting to old habits the moment things get busy.

Ninety days is the answer because it is long enough to build real skill and short enough to maintain focus. Research on habit formation consistently shows that sustained practice over roughly three months creates lasting behavioral change. Less than that produces temporary experiments. More than that without structure produces drift.

This plan divides the ninety days into three phases. Each phase has a specific focus, a set of weekly actions, and a checkpoint at the end. The phases are designed to build on each other. Do not skip ahead. The observation work in Month One makes the experimentation in Month Two possible. The experimentation in Month Two makes the habit-building in Month Three stick.

One more thing before you start. Do not try to work on all five dimensions simultaneously. Pick two. The two that scored lowest on your self-assessment, or the two that you believe will have the most immediate impact on your current role. Focus creates results. Breadth creates frustration.

Month One: Observe and Map

The first thirty days are not about changing anything. They are about seeing clearly.

Most developers have never systematically observed how their organization actually works. They know their immediate team. They understand their codebase. They have opinions about the processes they participate in. But they have not mapped the decision-making landscape, the communication patterns, or the influence dynamics that determine what gets built and why.

This month, your job is to map those things.

Week One. Identify the five most important decisions that will affect your team in the next quarter. For each decision, write down: who will make it, what information they need, who influences them, and where you currently sit in that chain. If you do not know the answer to any of these questions, that is your first data point. You are operating without visibility into the decisions that shape your work.

Week Two. Track every meeting you attend. For each one, note: was a decision made? Who spoke the most? Who spoke the least but had the most influence? What information was missing? After a week of this, you will have a clear picture of how your organization actually makes decisions versus how it thinks it makes decisions. Those two things are rarely the same.

Week Three. Have three conversations with people outside your immediate team. A product manager, a designer, someone from a different engineering team. Ask them the same question: what is the biggest challenge you are facing right now that engineering could help with? Listen to their answers. Do not solve their problems. Just listen and write down what you hear. You are building a map of organizational needs that your technical skills could address but currently are not.

Week Four. Review everything you have collected. Sit down with a blank page and an hour of uninterrupted time. Look for patterns. Where are the decision-making bottlenecks? Where is communication breaking down between teams? Where is good technical work being undermined by poor organizational alignment? Write a one-page summary of what you have observed.

Checkpoint. At the end of Month One, you should have a stakeholder map, a decision-making map, and a list of organizational gaps where you could add value beyond your current technical scope. If you do not have these things, spend another week on observation before moving to Month Two.

The Observation Trap

A warning before you move to Month Two. Some developers get comfortable in the observation phase. Mapping feels productive. It is analytical. It generates insights. It does not require you to do anything that feels risky or uncomfortable.

If you find yourself wanting to extend Month One, recognize that impulse for what it is. It is the same instinct that makes developers over-research before writing code. At some point, additional observation produces diminishing returns and the real learning only happens through action. Four weeks of observation is enough. Move on.

Month Two: Experiment and Practice

Now you change things. But carefully.

The goal of Month Two is to run small experiments in the two dimensions you chose. Each experiment should be low-risk, observable, and completable within a week. You are not trying to transform yourself. You are trying to practice specific skills in real situations and observe what happens.

Week Five. Run your first communication experiment. Take a complex technical topic your team is working on and write a one-paragraph explanation for a non-technical stakeholder. Share it with someone who fits that description and ask: does this make sense? Could you make a decision based on this? Their feedback will teach you more about communication effectiveness than any chapter in any book.

Week Six. Run your first influence experiment. Identify a decision that is coming up in the next two weeks. Before the meeting where that decision will be discussed, have a conversation with one key stakeholder to understand their perspective and share yours. Attend the meeting and notice the difference. Did having that pre-conversation change the dynamic? Did you feel more prepared? Did the stakeholder reference your earlier conversation?

Week Seven. Run your first people leadership experiment. If you manage someone, change the format of your next one-on-one. Instead of status updates, ask: what is one thing I could do differently that would make your work easier? If you do not manage anyone, give one piece of direct, specific, constructive feedback to a peer about their work. Not in writing. In conversation.

Week Eight. Run your first strategic thinking experiment. Before your next planning session, write down the three outcomes that matter most for the next sprint or cycle. Not tasks. Outcomes. Bring this to the planning session and frame the prioritization discussion around outcomes rather than ticket completion. Notice how the conversation changes.

Checkpoint. At the end of Month Two, review your experiments. Which ones felt natural? Which ones felt uncomfortable? The uncomfortable ones are the ones you need the most practice with. Which experiments produced visible results? Those are the ones to repeat and expand in Month Three.

What If the Experiments Fail?

They might. Some of your communication experiments will land flat. Some of your influence experiments will feel awkward. Some of your feedback conversations will not go the way you hoped.

This is normal and useful. A failed experiment is still a data point. It tells you something about the skill you are developing, about the organizational context you are operating in, or about how the other person received your approach. The only wasted experiment is one you do not reflect on.

When an experiment does not work, ask three questions. Was the approach wrong, the timing wrong, or the audience wrong? The answer tells you what to adjust for the next attempt. Leadership skills are refined through iteration, not through getting it right on the first try.

Month Three: Build Systems and Habits

The first two months were about awareness and experimentation. Month Three is about converting successful experiments into repeatable habits and building systems that sustain them.

The difference between a skill and a habit is consistency. A skill is something you can do when you decide to. A habit is something you do without deciding. Month Three builds the bridge between the two.

Week Nine. Take the experiments that worked in Month Two and turn them into weekly commitments. If the pre-meeting stakeholder conversation worked, commit to doing it before every important meeting. If the outcome-framing exercise changed your planning sessions, make it a permanent part of your preparation. Write these commitments down and put them where you will see them every Monday morning.

Week Ten. Start your decision log if you have not already. Record every significant decision you make or influence this week. Include what you decided, what information you had, what you were uncertain about, and what you would do differently in hindsight. Review the log at the end of each week. Patterns will emerge that tell you more about your decision-making tendencies than months of abstract reflection.

Week Eleven. Share what you have learned. Find an opportunity to help another developer who is earlier in their leadership transition. This could be a formal mentoring relationship, a casual conversation, or simply sharing the frameworks from this book that have been most useful to you. Teaching something is the fastest way to solidify your own understanding of it.

Week Twelve. Retake the self-assessment from earlier in this book. Compare your results to your original scores. Where have you improved? Where are you still stuck? Use the comparison to set priorities for the next ninety days.

Checkpoint. At the end of Month Three, you should have at least three new habits that you practice weekly without having to remind yourself. You should have a decision log with at least eight weeks of entries. You should have a clearer picture of the leader you are becoming and the specific areas that need continued development.

After the Ninety Days

The ninety-day plan ends but the work does not. Leadership development is not a project with a completion date. It is a practice that evolves as your role, your organization, and the industry change around you.

After completing this plan, set new goals for the next quarter. Pick different dimensions to focus on, or go deeper on the ones you started with. Revisit the self-assessment every six months. Update your stakeholder map when your organizational context changes. Keep the decision log running.

The developers who build these practices into their operating rhythm consistently outperform the ones who rely on talent and instinct alone. Not because the practices are magic. Because they force regular reflection, intentional improvement, and accountability to yourself.

There will be weeks when you slip. When the sprint is on fire and the exercises feel like a luxury you cannot afford. That is normal. The point is not perfection. The point is returning to the practice after the disruption passes. The developers who build lasting leadership capability are not the ones who never miss a week. They are the ones who always come back.

You started this book because something in the industry shifted and you felt it. You have spent the last ten chapters learning what to do about it. You have a self-assessment that tells you where you stand. You have exercises that build specific skills. And now you have a plan that turns all of it into action.

The gap between the developer you are today and the leader you can become is not about talent or intelligence or natural charisma. It is about practice. Deliberate, consistent, uncomfortable practice sustained over time.

The industry is going to keep changing. AI is going to keep improving. The roles and expectations that define your career are going to keep evolving. You cannot control any of that. What you can control is whether you develop the capabilities that make you valuable regardless of what the technology does next.

That is the real security. Not in any specific skill or tool or language. In the ability to lead, communicate, decide, and influence in any environment. Those capabilities do not deprecate. They compound.

Start Monday.

APPENDIX C

Frameworks Quick Reference

How to Use This Reference

This appendix collects every framework, template, and model from the book into one place. It is designed to be a quick-reference tool you can return to without rereading entire chapters.

Each framework is listed with its source chapter, a brief description, and the key components. For deeper context and examples, refer back to the original chapter.

The Four-Question Strategic Filter (Chapter 2)

Before starting any project or feature, answer these four questions in order.

What outcome are we trying to produce? Not what are we building. What change are we trying to create for the user, the business, or the organization?

Why does this outcome matter now? What has changed that makes this the right investment of engineering time? If nothing has changed, question whether the work is truly a priority or simply momentum.

What is the simplest path to this outcome? Not the most elegant architecture or the most comprehensive solution. The simplest thing that produces the desired result. Start there and iterate.

How will we know if we succeeded? Define the metric or observable behavior that tells you the outcome was achieved. If you cannot define this, the work is not ready to start.

The Three Levels of Communication (Chapter 3)

Every communication situation calls for one of three levels. Choosing the wrong level is the most common communication failure among technical leaders.

Level One: Technical Precision. Used with engineering peers. Full technical detail, specific language, no simplification. The goal is accuracy and completeness. The listener has the context to process the information as you present it.

Level Two: Contextual Translation. Used with product managers, designers, and cross-functional partners. Technical content translated into terms that connect to their priorities. Trade-offs framed in terms of user impact, timelines, and resource allocation rather than implementation details.

Level Three: Executive Compression. Used with senior leadership. Three things: what is happening, why it matters, and what you need from them. No more. Executives make dozens of decisions daily. Your job is to make their decision easy, not to educate them on your domain.

The Feedback Framework (Chapter 4)

Effective feedback follows a specific structure that separates observation from judgment and focuses on behavior rather than character.

Observation. Describe the specific behavior you observed. Not an interpretation. Not a feeling. The observable action. "In the last two code reviews, you approved the changes within five minutes of them being submitted."

Impact. Describe the concrete effect of that behavior. "Two of those changes introduced bugs that the QA team caught three days later, which pushed the release back."

Request. State what you would like to see instead. "I would like you to spend at least fifteen minutes on each review and leave at least one substantive comment per file."

The framework works because it removes ambiguity. The person receiving the feedback knows exactly what they did, why it mattered, and what to do differently.

The One-on-One Template (Chapter 4)

Replace status updates with three questions that surface real information.

What is the most frustrating part of your current work? This reveals obstacles, process problems, and emotional state in a single question.

What would you change about how the team operates if you could change one thing? This surfaces systemic issues that individuals rarely raise on their own.

Is there something you have been wanting to tell me but have not? This creates space for concerns that do not fit into any other conversation format.

Listen more than you talk. Take notes. Follow up on what you hear in the next session.

The Second-Order Effects Map (Chapter 5)

Before making a significant technical decision, map its effects at three levels.

First-order effects. The direct, immediate consequences of the decision. These are the ones everyone sees.

Second-order effects. The consequences of those consequences. The team that now has to change their integration. The monitoring alert that will fire differently. The deployment pipeline that gains a new dependency.

Third-order effects. The behavioral changes that result from second-order effects. The team that starts routing around your service because the integration became harder. The on-call engineer who starts ignoring a noisy alert.

Most technical decisions are evaluated only at the first-order level. Leaders evaluate at all three.

The Decision Classification Matrix (Chapter 6)

Every decision falls into one of four quadrants based on two dimensions: reversibility and impact.

Low impact, easily reversible. Make these immediately. Do not schedule meetings or gather additional data. The cost of delay exceeds the cost of being wrong.

Low impact, hard to reverse. Make these within a week. Gather minimal input from the people most affected, then decide.

High impact, easily reversible. Make these quickly but communicate clearly. The stakes are real but the ability to course-correct reduces the need for certainty.

High impact, hard to reverse. These are the only decisions that justify extensive analysis, multiple perspectives, and deliberate slowness. Most organizations treat every decision as if it falls in this quadrant. It does not. Learning to classify decisions correctly is what separates fast teams from slow ones.

The Stakeholder Map (Chapter 7)

For every major initiative, identify five things about each key stakeholder.

What do they care about most? Not what they say they care about. What their behavior reveals they prioritize.

What are they worried about? Every stakeholder has anxieties about how your work might affect their domain. Knowing those anxieties lets you address them proactively.

How do they prefer to receive information? Some want a document. Some want a conversation. Some want data. Delivering in their preferred format dramatically increases your influence.

Who influences them? Stakeholders are influenced by other people. Knowing who shapes their thinking gives you an indirect channel when the direct one is blocked.

When was the last time you talked to them? If the answer is more than two weeks ago for a critical stakeholder, your influence is fading. Relationships require maintenance.

The Three Delegation Buckets (Chapter 8)

Sort every task on your plate into one of three categories.

Only I can do this. Tasks that require your specific judgment, relationships, or authority. These should be no more than 40 percent of your workload.

Someone else could do this with guidance. Tasks where you provide context, define success criteria, and then step back. Delegation here develops the person taking the task and frees your time.

Someone else could do this better than me. Tasks where another person has more skill, more context, or more capacity. Delegating these is not about offloading. It is about putting work in the hands of the person best equipped to do it well.

If the first bucket contains more than half your work, you are holding too much. If the third bucket is empty, you are not leveraging your team effectively.

The Four Communication Templates (Chapter 8)

Template One: The Status Update. What we did. What we learned. What comes next. Three sentences maximum.

Template Two: The Trade-off Presentation. We have two options. Option A gives us this benefit at this cost. Option B gives us this benefit at this cost. We recommend Option B because of this reason. What questions do you have?

Template Three: The Escalation. Here is the problem. Here is the impact if we do not address it. Here is what I recommend. Here is what I need from you to make it happen.

Template Four: The Alignment Check. Here is what I believe we agreed to. Here is what I am planning to do based on that agreement. If I have this wrong, please tell me by this date.

Each template serves a different communication need. The skill is not in the template itself. It is in recognizing which situation calls for which template.

The Visibility Framework (Chapter 8)

Share your team's work with one person outside your immediate team every week. Use this format.

What we accomplished. One or two sentences about the concrete output.

Why it matters. One sentence connecting the work to an outcome that the audience cares about.

What comes next. One sentence about what the work enables or what the next step is.

Do this consistently for three months. The compound effect on how your team and your work are perceived will be significant.

APPENDIX D

Annotated Reading List

About This List

These books shaped the thinking behind this one. Each recommendation is organized by the chapter themes it complements, with a brief note on what it adds beyond what this book covers.

This is not a comprehensive reading list. It is a curated one. Every book here earned its place by being useful in practice, not just interesting in theory. If you read three books from this list over the next year, alongside the exercises in this book, you will have a stronger foundation than most developers who spend that same year reading blog posts and watching conference talks.

A note on ordering: within each section, the books are listed in order of practical immediacy. The first book in each section is the one I would recommend reading first if you are focused on that dimension. The others are valuable but can wait until you have absorbed and practiced the core ideas.

Strategic Thinking (Chapters 1 and 2)

The Effective Executive by Peter Drucker. Written in 1966 and still the clearest articulation of what it means to work on the right things instead of just working hard. Drucker's insight that effectiveness can be learned is the foundation of the strategic shift this book describes. Short, direct, and free of the filler that plagues modern business books.

Good Strategy Bad Strategy by Richard Rumelt. Most organizations confuse goals with strategy. Rumelt explains the difference with painful clarity. If you want to understand why so many product roadmaps fail despite everyone working hard, this book provides the structural explanation.

An Elegant Puzzle by Will Larson. The most practical book written about engineering management and organizational design. Larson addresses the specific challenges of scaling engineering teams with a level of detail that most leadership books avoid. Essential reading for anyone moving into a role where they influence how teams are structured.

Communication (Chapter 3)

Thinking in Systems by Donella Meadows. Despite the title, this book is as much about communication as it is about systems. Meadows demonstrates how to explain complex interdependencies in clear, accessible language. Reading it will improve both your systems thinking and your ability to communicate systemic ideas to non-technical audiences.

The Pyramid Principle by Barbara Minto. The standard reference for structured communication in professional contexts. Minto's approach of leading with the conclusion and supporting with evidence runs counter to how most engineers communicate, which is exactly why it is worth studying.

On Writing Well by William Zinsser. Not a business book. A book about clear writing that applies to every written communication you produce. Zinsser's principles of simplicity, clarity, and cutting unnecessary words will improve your emails, documents, and proposals immediately.

People Leadership (Chapter 4)

The Manager's Path by Camille Fournier. The definitive guide for technical professionals moving into management. Fournier covers the entire trajectory from tech lead to CTO with specific, honest advice about what each transition actually involves. If you read one management book, make it this one.

Radical Candor by Kim Scott. The best framework for understanding why feedback fails and how to deliver it effectively. Scott's two-by-two of caring personally and challenging directly resolves the tension most engineers feel between being honest and being kind.

Turn the Ship Around by L. David Marquet. A leadership book disguised as a Navy submarine story. Marquet's model of intent-based leadership, where the leader provides context and the team provides decisions, maps directly to how the best engineering teams operate.

Systems Thinking and Decision-Making (Chapters 5 and 6)

Thinking, Fast and Slow by Daniel Kahneman. The definitive work on how human judgment fails under uncertainty. Every decision-making bias described in Chapter 6 is explored in depth here. Dense but essential for anyone who wants to understand why smart people make predictable mistakes.

The Goal by Eliyahu Goldratt. Written as a novel about a manufacturing plant, but the theory of constraints it introduces applies directly to software systems and engineering organizations. If you have ever wondered why optimizing one part of your system made the whole thing slower, Goldratt explains why.

Thinking in Bets by Annie Duke. A practical guide to making decisions when the outcome is uncertain. Duke's framework for separating decision quality from outcome quality is particularly useful for technical leaders who need to make calls without complete information.

Influence and Organizational Dynamics (Chapters 7 and 8)

Influence by Robert Cialdini. The foundational text on how persuasion works. Cialdini identifies the specific mechanisms that cause people to say yes, and understanding those mechanisms makes you both a more effective influencer and a better detector of when others are influencing you.

Staff Engineer by Will Larson. A companion to An Elegant Puzzle focused specifically on the individual contributor leadership path. Larson describes the archetypes, expectations, and strategies for operating at the staff-plus level, where influence without authority is the primary mode of getting things done.

The First 90 Days by Michael Watkins. Originally written for executives transitioning into new roles, but the frameworks apply to any significant career transition. The emphasis on early wins, stakeholder mapping, and building credibility maps directly to the transition from developer to leader.

The Future of Technical Work (Chapter 9)

Team Topologies by Matthew Skelton and Manuel Pais. The best current framework for thinking about how engineering organizations should be structured. As AI changes what individual developers can accomplish, the way teams are organized becomes the primary lever for organizational effectiveness.

The Mythical Man-Month by Frederick Brooks. Written in 1975 and still accurate about why adding people to a late project makes it later. Brooks understood that the hard problems in software are communication and coordination, not computation. That insight is more relevant now than ever.

Accelerate by Nicole Forsgren, Jez Humble, and Gene Kim. The research-backed case for how engineering practices drive organizational performance. If you ever need to make a data-driven argument for investing in technical excellence, this book provides the evidence.

Where to Start

If the list feels overwhelming, here are three starting points based on common profiles.

If your self-assessment showed communication as your weakest dimension, start with The Pyramid Principle. It will immediately improve every document, email, and presentation you produce.

If people leadership is your biggest gap, start with The Manager's Path. Fournier's progression from tech lead to senior leader mirrors the transition this book describes, and her advice is specific enough to act on immediately.

If you rated strongest in technical skills but weakest in organizational awareness, start with An Elegant Puzzle. Larson writes about engineering leadership the way engineers think, with systems, frameworks, and data. It will feel familiar even as it stretches your perspective.

ABOUT THE AUTHOR

About the Author

Enrique Somoza, D.Sc., is a product and technology leader with over a decade of experience building and scaling enterprise software and internet infrastructure. He has led product strategy for large-scale distributed systems, including global DNS platforms that handle a significant portion of internet traffic.

He began his career as a developer, building a deep technical foundation in systems, performance, and architecture. Over time, his role evolved beyond writing code into leading cross-functional teams, shaping product direction, and driving decisions at scale. That transition from hands-on engineer to product and business leader is the foundation of this book.

Dr. Somoza holds a D.Sc. in Cybersecurity, where his research focused on detecting and mitigating DNS-based attacks using data-driven and AI-assisted approaches. His work bridges the gap between technical systems and real-world impact, combining engineering depth with strategic thinking.

Throughout his career, he has worked closely with engineering, product, and executive teams to solve complex problems, align organizations, and deliver scalable solutions. He has seen firsthand that the most impactful technical professionals are not just strong engineers, but strong communicators, decision-makers, and leaders.

He wrote this book to help developers stay relevant as the industry shifts beyond code.

www.ingramcontent.com/pod-product-compliance
Lightning Source LLC
LaVergne TN
LVHW060037210926
848481LV00013B/3887